Change Your Mindset to Achieve Success

The Ultimate Guide to Eliminate Self-Doubt, Build Confidence, and Turn Your Dreams Into Reality

Ale A. Heinen

Table of Contents

Introduction

Success is not an accident, success is actually a choice. –Stephen Curry

I don't know how many times I have failed to finish a workout program. I would start off very excited and motivated to create a healthier version of myself. I would do really well in the first four or five days. But then, life would get in the way...

I would get "'busy" and make up all kinds of excuses as to why I couldn't work out that day. And then the next, and the next, only to wake up one day and realize I haven't worked out in weeks. Once again, I had quit on myself. I would feel like a total failure.

To break my self-esteem down even more, I fell into the trap of comparing myself to other people who seemed to have it all together. I would start doubting myself and my own capabilities. The more I struggled with self-doubt, the more I felt incompetent and like I would never achieve any of my goals.

One day, after taking a good look at myself and my life, I came to the realization that things had to change, starting with my mindset. When I am faced with a challenge and fail, I can either learn from it and grow, or I could quit, feel sorry for myself, and ultimately stop trying altogether (which I had been doing). I also recognized the importance of finding greatness and motivation in the small things: Like getting a chore out of the way as early as possible every day or meeting a small milestone on a big project.

Those small achievements made a difference in my motivation and my eagerness to do what I needed to do in order to attain success. My life didn't change overnight, and it wasn't always easy. I had to be willing to work hard for what I wanted and not give up and fail again. But, with one small step at a time, I was able to change my mindset by gaining confidence in myself and my abilities. This helped me, and I know it can help you too.

Your story may sound different from mine. It may be that you are afraid to get out of your comfort zone because you believe you don't have the qualifications to do so or that you believe you will fail before you even start. It may be that there was a time when you had big dreams for your future, but after facing a few challenges, you have forgotten about your own capabilities and strengths.

It may be that you feel blinded by the pressures of society and the images of yourself painted by you or others. It may be that you feel defeated because a promotion or career advancement seems out of your reach. It may be that in your personal life you struggle to build proper connections with others, unconsciously seeking out toxic relationships. *The list could go on—you are not alone.* It is estimated that around 86% of people (adults and adolescents) struggle due to low self-esteem (Guttman, 2019).

The good news is that you can break free from the shackles that have resulted in you becoming a prisoner of your own negative thoughts. I have been in this position too. You can learn to change your mindset by changing your thoughts: focusing on growth, rebuilding confidence, and embracing failures. This is exactly what *Change Your Mindset to Achieve Success* will help you with. What's more, you will also learn how to assess yourself, reflect on your mistakes, and draft a plan that outlines what needs to be done. This will help you feel more confident and capable of achieving your goals.

As a Division I golf coach, I've always been fascinated by the different mindsets our student-athletes have and their impact on their development. The ones who excel the most are the ones who are willing to learn and grow. The ones with a growth mindset don't mind trying new and uncomfortable things. They aren't afraid of failure because their self-worth is not attached to it.

Most people set mental boundaries that prevent them from reaching success. Why are we so afraid to change? Sometimes we aren't even aware that our way of thinking isn't leading us to our dreams. When this is the case, we need to purposefully change our mindsets to gear ourselves for success. With this book, I hope to inspire people to make the necessary changes to their mindset. By training your mind to think correctly, you can achieve success in any area of your life. Yes, you may struggle at times—and that's okay—but soon you will realize the incredible power that lies within you. The power to change your life is in your hands (and mind).

If you have the correct mindset and believe in yourself, you are capable of overcoming whatever odds may be stacked against you, much like boxing champion Muhammad Ali. When he started his boxing career, he failed all the tests that assess a boxer's skills. He wasn't a natural fighter, and not many people believed in his abilities. But he had the mindset of a champion. He believed in himself to such an extent that it didn't matter to him if others didn't have the same faith in him. This helped him rise above all his competitors to become one of the greatest boxers in history.

Once you're able to change your mindset, you may even realize that your fears in life were completely unfounded. Let's look at the singer, dancer, and actress Jennifer Lopez. Even though her dream had always been to be a singer, she was insecure about her voice and didn't think she was good enough to make it a career. She was also insecure about being judged by others. However, she changed her mindset and overcame her insecurities by reminding herself that she was the only one standing in the way of her achieving her goals and realizing her potential.

Whether you are like Mohammad Ali, who faced others who doubted him, or like Jennifer, who faced self-doubts, when you go step by step with me through *Change Your Mindset to Achieve Success,* you will be equipped with the right mindset for your journey to a new, successful you.

So, let's get started by discussing what it means to be successful and why it can be so difficult to achieve the success that you desire.

Chapter 1:

Why Is It So Hard to

Become Successful?

Happiness depends on your mindset and attitude. –Roy T. Bennet

Have you ever met a person who simply doesn't want to achieve any form of success? Not in a single aspect of their lives? I haven't, and I'm going to take the guess that you haven't either. I believe it's fairly safe to say that everyone wants to be successful. Yes, their idea of success may be different from yours, but they still have dreams and goals that they would deeply like to reach, whether on a personal or professional level.

Now, ask yourself this question: If everyone wants to have a successful life, why is it so difficult to reach this goal? A recent poll showed that 90% of people who try to improve themselves or strive for success fail (Rao, 2017). If you don't believe me, think back to the start of every new year. Wherever you go toward the end of December or the beginning of January, you'll find people making and talking about their New Year's resolutions.

How many of these people actually follow through on these?

While there are many reasons why your resolutions or other plans don't work out—such as setting unrealistic goals or not truly wanting what you try to achieve—many times it comes down to not creating the correct mindset to truly go for your goals.

Not being aware of your mindset and taking the necessary steps to improve it can result in extremely limiting beliefs—such as the belief that you're not good enough to achieve success—as well as poor self-esteem. The good news is that if you work on improving your mindset, you can achieve the success you desire. It all starts with developing a deep understanding of the impact a poor mindset can have on your life and then taking the necessary steps to not only become more aware of your mindset but also how to improve it to create a growth mindset.

Poor Self-Esteem

Let's start by discussing self-esteem and how it can affect you. Self-esteem has to do with the way you see yourself and the value you attach to yourself. When you have good self-esteem, you will believe that you're capable of anything you put your mind to and that nothing will get you down. However, if you have bad self-esteem, you may struggle to complete even the simplest of tasks, believing that you have failed before you even try.

Self-esteem goes beyond simply affecting how you complete a task. It affects you in all of the following ways:

- how you assert yourself

- your ability to make decisions

- the value you place on yourself

- your willingness to try new things

- your ability to recognize your strengths

- the kindness you show yourself

- how you cope with making mistakes

- the extent of the guilt you feel when you do something wrong

- the level of happiness you believe you deserve

- how you practice self-care

- whether you believe in yourself

Since your self-esteem can have a massive impact on various aspects of your life, it's important to become more aware of how you feel about yourself so that you can take action to improve your self-esteem whenever you need to. Typical signs of low self-esteem include:

- **Poor confidence**: Low self-esteem and low self-confidence go hand-in-hand. While self-esteem is about how you value yourself, self-confidence is about your trust in yourself. They both contribute to each other and are a consequence of each other's presence. When your confidence is low, you will struggle to believe in yourself or trust in your own abilities. This can severely affect your overall well-being, as you won't trust that you're able to navigate the various problems you may encounter in your life. Always be mindful of your levels of confidence, and if you become aware of them dropping, work on gaining trust in yourself again. Ways to do this can include reminding yourself of a previous time you were able to solve a specific problem or learn a new skill.

- **Lack of control**: When you have low self-esteem, you may feel like you have no control over your life. You may feel like no changes you make to your life will be effective or give you the control you need, so there's no point in even trying. As much as there may always be aspects of your life that you can't control, it's important that you learn to differentiate between what you can control and what you can't and choose to focus on the aspects that you can change.

Creating this mindset where you direct your focus effectively will be life-changing.

- **Making negative social comparisons**: If you have low self-esteem, you may constantly find yourself comparing yourself to others who you believe are more successful than you are. This is often referred to as upward comparisons, where you compare yourself only to people who you believe are better than you, never to your peers. While these types of comparisons can be a fantastic motivating tool to push yourself to higher levels of success, they can also break you down, particularly if you don't believe you are truly capable of reaching these goals. Become more aware of who you compare yourself to and be more wary of using what people post on social media when you make these comparisons. People's social media accounts are rarely a true reflection of what happens in their lives.

- **Not asking for what you need**: When you don't believe you deserve true happiness or success, you may not believe that you are entitled to ask for what you need in life. This can be when you need help with something or even support when you are going through a difficult time. When you need to ask for help or support, you may feel embarrassed, as you will make it clear to others that you don't have control over every aspect of your life. This embarrassment can drop your self-esteem even more, resulting in you neglecting your own needs and desires even more.

- **Self-doubt and second-guessing**: When you have low self-esteem, you may struggle to make decisions, and even after you've spent hours (if not more) deliberating over and second-guessing even the smallest details of a decision, you may be hit with extreme self-doubt or worry the minute after you've made your decision. The less trust you have in your own abilities, the more your self-esteem will suffer.

- **Difficulty accepting feedback**: When you struggle with low self-esteem, you may have extreme difficulty accepting any form of feedback, whether positive or negative. When you listen to negative feedback, your self-esteem will most probably drop even lower. Positive feedback can be just as difficult to hear. You may doubt whether the feedback is truly positive, wonder if people have ulterior motives, or think that the person isn't being truthful in their feedback.

- **Negative self-talk**: It can be difficult to be kind to yourself and have positive thoughts and self-talk when you have low self-esteem. Instead, you may beat yourself up even more with your negative thoughts and self-talk, lowering your self-esteem even more. Become more aware when you have negative thoughts or talk to yourself in a bad way. Then, make an active effort to change these negatives into positives. You can even tell yourself something like, "I will not allow negativity to take over my life," after which you replace any negative thoughts and words with positive ones. Do this continuously, and you will soon experience more positive results in your life.

- **Fear of failure**: When you have low self-esteem, it can be difficult to focus on your own strengths rather than your flaws. Over time, you may get so used to focusing on your weaknesses that you even forget about your strengths. This can drop your self-esteem even more, as you won't believe that you have the skills and abilities to do things. However, if you think back, you'll remember the many times you solved problems or completed tasks with ease. If you could succeed then, you can again.

- **Lack of boundaries**: If you don't believe you're worthy or deserving of success or happiness, you may find it difficult to set healthy boundaries to protect yourself physically, mentally, or emotionally. You may even feel guilty about setting specific boundaries meant to protect you.

However, the more people overstep and violate the boundaries you want to set, the more your self-esteem will drop. Consider what boundaries you would like to set in your life and start by setting an easy one. This will give you the confidence you may need to set more goals.

- **Wanting to please others**: If you constantly go out of your way to try to make others happy, especially if this is at a cost to your own well-being, you may have low self-esteem. When you please others, you gain extra validation that will help you feel good about yourself. However, if you constantly neglect your own needs to make someone else happy, you will neglect your own happiness. When someone asks you to do something that you don't feel comfortable with or that will go against fulfilling your own needs, try to say "no." Initially, it can be very difficult to do this, but the more you say "no," the easier it will become.

While we've already touched on some of the more obvious consequences of low self-esteem, its impact can go much deeper than struggling to prioritize your own needs or being unable to complete tasks. It can also negatively affect your mental health. Low self-esteem is directly linked to these mental health conditions:

- anxiety disorders

- depression

- emotional distress

- panic disorders

- addictions

- eating disorders

- stress

- suicidal ideations

Many of these conditions can leave you feeling extremely sad and despondent. When you act on these feelings and show others how sad you are, you may get the support you need. However, you should steer clear of allowing this to become a crutch that keeps you from moving forward. Instead, you have the power within you to overcome any challenges you may have with low self-esteem and reach your goals.

There are many different reasons why people struggle with low self-esteem. Understanding these reasons can help you address the cause and not just the symptoms. While some personality types tend to question their own self-worth more, mental health conditions can also be the cause of low self-esteem.

Other reasons include

- obsessing over very specific things

- low levels of resilience

- ineffective coping skills

- being overly critical of yourself

- perfectionism

- physical health problems

To achieve the goals and success you dream, you need to work on improving your self-esteem. If you don't believe you can reach your goals, you will actively look for excuses, whether they are valid or not. However, if you have confidence in your own abilities and know you can achieve anything you set your mind to, half the battle will already be won.

Success and self-esteem also feed off each other. The more your self-esteem improves, the more success you will achieve. And, the more goals you reach, the more you will believe in your own abilities. If you're able to build your self-esteem to get into this positive cycle, you will be capable of achieving anything you put your mind to. What's more, you'll also feel happier in all aspects of your life.

On the flip side, if your self-esteem is low, especially when you've created limiting beliefs such as you're not good enough to do something, you will actively seek out more negativity in your life, whether consciously or subconsciously. Your mind will seek out validation every day to prove that your limiting belief is true. For example, if you've created a limiting belief that you're not good enough and a colleague comes up with a solution to a problem before you could, you'll see this as validation that you really aren't good enough. What's more, your limiting belief most likely kept you from thinking outside the box to find the solution, as you may have believed that someone else would come up with a better solution than you could, so there would be no point in even trying.

Luckily, it's possible to let go of these limiting beliefs and their effect on your self-esteem. If you change what you allow your brain to focus on, you can reduce the power that your limiting beliefs have in your life. One way of doing this is by consistently repeating positive mantras or affirmations specifically directed at addressing the limiting belief that has been keeping you back. This is most effective when you say these words out loud, as your brain reacts differently to things that you say than to things that you simply think. The more you repeat this mantra, the more your brain will start to accept it as the truth, and as such, it will remove the power that this limiting belief once had over your life.

Before we go into more detail about how you can do this, think about your life and the limiting beliefs you may have. This can be anything from believing that you can't make proper decisions, that you're not worthy of having healthy relationships, or that you're not as good as others. You may have a few limiting beliefs that are holding you back. Write all of them down on a piece of paper.

Once you have a list of limiting beliefs written down, prioritize them according to the ones that have the biggest impact on your life. Also, consider what you would most like to change and, as a result, what would have the biggest positive influence on your life if you changed it. After you create your new list of priorities, identify one that you would like to work on first. You may be tempted to go for the one that will have the biggest impact on your life. However, since this limiting belief will likely have emotional consequences, it may be easier for you to start with a smaller belief that may not have big emotional roots. Overcoming this smaller, limiting belief first will also give you the confidence to take on the bigger, more impactful beliefs.

Now, take the limiting belief that you want to address first and imagine how your life would be if it were no longer part of it. Let's say you want to address your lack of confidence. This can be your confidence in life in general or, more specifically, in your personal or professional lives. Now, think of how your life would be if you had more confidence, and then design a mantra that will help you break these limiting beliefs. To help you with this exercise, here are some examples that you can either apply in your life or help you develop your own mantra (Marcus, 2017):

Life without your limiting belief	Mantra to reinforce your confidence
If I were more confident, I would be in a role I enjoy, doing work I enjoy, and growing in my profession.	I believe in my ability to find and succeed in a fulfilling career.
If I were more confident, I'd allow myself to make mistakes and learn lessons from them.	I'm open to trying something new, and I'm confident that I can learn from this experience, whatever the outcome.
If I were more confident, I'd ask questions, listen, and respond in an objective way. Because I'm worried, I won't say the right thing, I say nothing.	I'm smart and thoughtful, and I have a lot to contribute to my team and the organization.
If I were more confident, I would be clear and direct in my communication and not use minimizing language or find ways to soften my statements.	I'm confident in my ability to communicate clearly and directly with others.

If I were more confident, I'd question myself a whole lot less.	I take positive action on behalf of others as well as myself.
If I were more confident, I'd be less defensive and more open to receiving constructive feedback. In fact, I'd ask for it on a regular basis.	I value feedback from others, and I'm open to receiving feedback in order to grow professionally.
If I were more confident, I wouldn't be consumed by the thought that everyone else is smarter and more successful than I am or view their success as a mark against my self-worth.	I have the talent to reach my full potential, and I celebrate the success of others as well as my own.
If I were more confident, I'd be happier, and my relationships would be healthier.	I deserve to be happy in my relationships with other people and enjoy the support of loved ones.

Once you've decided on the mantra you want to use in your life, say it out loud as often as you can, particularly when you're feeling stressed or feel like the limiting belief is taking overpower in your life again. While in the beginning you may not feel any different after using these mantras, over time their power will become more apparent, and you will soon realize that these limiting beliefs will have no impact on your life anymore. You will start to understand that you're capable of amazing things, and as a result, your self-esteem will improve.

Cognitive Biases

Apart from limiting beliefs and low self-esteem, you may also struggle with cognitive biases that may be affecting the way you do things and the subsequent success you achieve. Cognitive biases are errors in the way you think that can hold you back from reaching your full potential. In psychology, these are often referred to as mental blind spots.

Once you know what cognitive biases you may have in your life, you'll have a much better understanding of how your mind, as well as the minds of others, work. This can help you determine ways you can adjust your behavior to increase the influence you have over other people.

Let's look at the most common cognitive biases that may be blocking your success:

- **Availability bias**: People are naturally more drawn to accept information that they can easily understand. That is why you may reject information that is too out-of-the-box, which can result in you missing out on taking calculated risks and achieving success. This often happens when information on new developments and technology becomes available before it has been tried, tested, and proven to be effective.

- **Status quo bias**: Many people struggle with accepting change and getting out of their comfort zones. As a result, they may prefer things to stay the same and for them to continue working the way they used to. Not getting out of your comfort zone may result in you not moving your career forward, as you may stay stuck in what you know and not be willing to take chances to improve your life. Business managers with a status quo bias may also keep their companies from being competitive, as others may take chances that they aren't willing to take. Unfortunately, in the current world that is constantly changing, you may take a bigger risk by staying with your status quo bias than you would if you tried something new.

- **Egocentric bias**: This is when you consider your point of view to be more important than those of others. You're unwilling to listen to the opinions of others because you believe you know better and that their input won't improve the outcome achieved. In the business world, egocentric bias can also be present when you focus too much on the information that supports your project and overlook any data that may conflict with it. This type of bias can lead you to make many mistakes in life, as you won't consider other viewpoints or information that may prove your ideas invalid.

- **Affect heuristic bias**: This type of bias takes place when you place a bigger focus on your emotional response to things than your cognitive processes. If you have an intense negative emotional reaction to something, you may be hesitant to take a chance and take action. Similarly, anything that provokes a positive emotional response will be enticing, while you may overlook anything that doesn't provide any form of emotional punch. This can result in new trends being overlooked or ignored because they don't cause an emotional reaction. By the time your emotions are triggered by it, you may have missed the golden opportunity to implement these trends.

- **Overconfidence bias**: This bias is very similar to the egocentric one. You believe you are always right and, as a result, don't want to surround yourself with people who disagree with you. You overestimate your own abilities. When people openly disagree with you, you may overreact and even try to force your own views on them.

Take some time to think about your own life and the cognitive biases you may have. Write them down on a sheet of paper and try to include specific instances where your cognitive biases have kept you from achieving your goals. This will help you easily identify where you tend to go wrong, which will make it easier for you to rectify your behavior.

Once you've evaluated your own biases, do the same for the people in your life. This includes any person—partner, parents, siblings, children, or friends—as well as those in your professional life, such as your manager, boss, and coworkers. If you can better understand how these people tend to think, you can adjust the way in which you try to work with them. For example, if your manager has egocentric biases, voicing your conflicting opinions out loud won't do you any favors. You'll need to consider taking a different approach; for example, subtly introduce your opinion so that they never feel assaulted by it and perhaps even start to believe that your opinion is, in fact, their own opinion.

The Two Mindsets

Working on improving your self-esteem and cognitive biases is a great tool for creating the perfect mindset where you are open to change and willing to take the necessary chances to reach your goals. Your mindset is all about your own belief in yourself, your abilities, and your qualities. If you have a healthy mindset, you will believe in yourself without becoming overly arrogant, which may push people who can propel you to success away.

Carol Dweck, a well-known American psychologist, spent many years doing various studies on mindsets and how to improve them. She concluded that there are two types of mindsets (Dweck, 2015):

- **Fixed mindset:** These are the people who believe that their abilities, which include their skills, intelligence, and talents, are fixed and that no matter what they do, they can't improve on what they're already capable of. As a result, they struggle with any form of change, don't like to be challenged, give up easily when they face difficulties, see all negative feedback as criticism, and feel threatened when other people achieve success. People with fixed mindsets almost never reach their full potential, as their mindsets are holding them back from going for their goals.

- **Growth mindset:** These are the people who believe that they are capable of doing anything that they set their minds to by working hard to develop new or improve existing skills. They are highly resilient and love to be challenged. They see failure as an opportunity to learn lessons and expand their knowledge. They seek out the positive in feedback, no matter how negative it may be. When they see someone else achieving success, they are inspired to improve themselves to reach the same goals.

It Starts in the Brain

You have the power within you to change your mindset. Whether you want to do a complete overhaul to go from a fixed mindset to a growing one or simply expand your existing growing mindset to help you achieve more success, you can do this. Doing this starts with becoming more aware of your thoughts, making a conscious decision not to listen to any negative thoughts you might have, and changing the way you react to your thoughts.

It all comes down to changing the way your mind—and therefore, your brain—works. When you make decisions, your brain creates and destroys neural pathways to tell your body what actions you should take. When you constantly make similar decisions, your brain's neural pathways not only become stronger but also easier to create. Over time, the neural pathways that you almost never use become weaker until they are eventually destroyed. To change your mindset, you have to force your brain to create new neural pathways and destroy the ones that haven't brought you the desired results in the past.

Here's some good news for you: By choosing to find better ways of achieving the success you desire and reading this book, you've already started the process of changing the existing neural pathways in your brain. The more you expose your mind to and implement the information and exercises in this book, the stronger these new neural pathways to an improved mindset will become. As these new pathways develop, you'll find it easier to believe in yourself, which will result in your brain becoming more willing to work on strengthening these pathways even more.

It all comes down to neuroplasticity and understanding its connection with creating a growth mindset. In layman's terms, neuroplasticity refers to your brain's ability to adapt and change. This typically happens in three stages:

- When you try to do something new, such as learning a new skill, there will be chemical changes happening in your brain.

- As you continue to work on perfecting your new skill, physical changes will take place in your brain. New pathways are created, and the actual structure of your brain may change.

- The more you practice this skill, the stronger your brain's association (or pathways) with it will become, and the easier you will be able to complete tasks using it.

As you're working on changing your mindset, remember that the changes that can happen in the brain can be positive or negative. If you don't fully commit to making positive changes, your new neural pathways won't be stimulated properly, and your previous pathways, which either created negative results or didn't bring you the success you desired, may take over again.

Research has shown that the best way to use your neuroplasticity to create a growth mindset is to create experience-based opportunities for your brain to learn and adapt (Silver, 2022). Think about what level of success you would like to achieve and what activities or experiences may help your brain develop the necessary neural pathways to get there. The more pleasant you can make these experiences, the easier it will be for you to build strong new pathways.

It is, however, important that you be patient with yourself and with this process. It will take time and consistent effort to develop these new pathways, especially if you want them to bring long-lasting results. However, the more you work on building these new pathways or growth mindsets, the easier it will get to change your behavior to bring you closer to the success you desire.

When you struggle and if you ever feel like giving up, remind yourself of how far you've come already, what you were able to achieve along the way, and what you hope to still achieve. If you deeply want to reach your goal and feel truly invested in the outcome, you will be able to push through any obstacles that you may face along the way. You simply have to believe in yourself and your own abilities.

Self-Assessment: What Is Your Mindset?

Let's take the next step in identifying and changing your mindset. Answer each of the questions truthfully by scoring each question from 0 to 3, with 0 being strongly agreeing and 3 being strongly disagreeing. Once you're done, you can calculate your totals. Remember, answering these questions honestly will help you reach success. You don't have to show your answers to anyone, so keep an open mind while you're busy with this assessment (*Carol Dweck's Growth versus Fixed Mindset Assessment*, n.d.):

		Score
1	Your level of intelligence is something you have no control over and can't change.	
2	Only certain people or cultures can excel at math.	
3	All people are actually good; some just make horrible mistakes and bad decisions.	
4	You can't change the type of person you are.	
5	You can change basic things about yourself without any problems.	
6	A new skill, such as playing a musical instrument, can be learned by anyone.	
7	You have to be born with a specific talent to excel at certain things, such as sports.	
8	You are able to change your intelligence as much as you want.	

9	The more you practice doing something, the easier it will get.	
10	No matter what type of person you are or what mistakes you've made in the past, you can change your future.	
11	I experience high levels of stress when I try something new, so I choose to avoid new things.	
12	Some people are good, while others are bad. There's nothing you can do to change this.	
13	I appreciate it when people give me feedback on my performance.	
14	I tend to get angry when I get negative feedback.	
15	All people—except those with traumatic brain injuries or deficits—are capable of the same amount of learning.	
16	While you can learn new skills, you can't increase your intelligence.	

17	While you can learn to do things differently, it won't change the type of person you are.	
18	You can always make changes to your level of intelligence.	
19	I enjoy learning new things.	
20	People who are highly intelligent don't have to try as hard as others with a lower IQ.	
Total		

Your grand total will give you a good indication of where your mindset is currently at:

45 to 60 points	Strong growth mindset
34 to 44 points	Growth mindset with some fixed ideas
21 to 31 points	Fixed mindset with some growth ideas
0 to 20 points	Strong fixed mindset

After you've been working on improving your mindset for a few weeks, feel free to redo this assessment to measure your progress and determine how much work you may still need to do to achieve a growing mindset.

Your mindset can either stand in your way of achieving the success you desire, or it can propel you to reach new heights. Think about the type of mindset you have—fixed or growing—and do whatever you can to improve it. This might mean working on your low self-esteem or cognitive biases that have been holding you back.

Always remember that you are capable of achieving greatness, and by simply changing your neural pathways, you will be well on your way to turning your dreams into a reality. To help you along this journey, we will now look at how you can identify the first thing you need to work on: acceptance of yourself.

Chapter 2:

What's the First Thing You

Need to Work On?

You can conquer almost any fear if you will only make up your mind to do so. Remember, fear doesn't exist anywhere except in the mind. –Dale Carnegie

While we've looked at the two mindsets people have and how this can impact your ability to achieve success, let's put this into practice and look at the story of John, a 42-year-old husband, and father of three. By his own definition, John achieved success in his career: He was the manager of the company he worked for.

His rise at the company happened quickly, and he attributes a lot of his career success to his perfectionism and willingness to do whatever is needed to complete tasks effectively and as close to perfect as is humanly possible. However, this often resulted in conflict, not only with other managers but also with the employees that reported to him. John chose not to let these conflicts bother him and instead focused on the outcomes.

One day, conflict between John and a fellow manager got out of hand, and the company instructed them both to attend sessions with a psychologist or risk facing serious consequences at work. John felt like he was being treated unfairly but attended because he couldn't afford to lose his job.

During his sessions, it was uncovered that John's perfectionism often resulted in him not trusting his employees, making them feel unappreciated and their work never good enough for him. The psychologist made John realize that, despite the success that he has achieved, he actually doesn't have a lot of faith in his ability to change the way he has always done things. He had a fixed mindset, not only in the abilities of others but also in his belief in himself.

After a few sessions, the psychologist made John realize that it was his fixed mindset, combined with his low self-esteem and perfectionism, that led him to be stressed for the last few years, and he needed medication to help him cope with it. With the psychologist's help, John started working on changing his mindset from fixed to growth, taking it step-by-step, starting with acknowledging his mindset. Next, John was taught how to accept himself, how to embrace change, and the importance of stepping outside your comfort zone to achieve the success you want. By doing this, John learned to trust his employees more and started to accept the opinions of others. Being more accommodating resulted in a more peaceful environment at work, and both John's and his team's performance improved drastically.

John was able to change his life by making the necessary changes to live the life he wanted. You can also achieve these types of results by taking the same steps he took to change his mindset, starting with acknowledging that you have a fixed mindset.

Acknowledge Your Fixed Mindset

The first step in changing your mindset is to admit that you have one. Once you acknowledge this to yourself openly and honestly, it will help you identify the various instances where your mindset kept you back in the past. For example, you can say something like, "My fixed mindset caused me not to believe in myself when I was up for a promotion. This resulted in me not giving my all and failing before I even tried to compete for the job." In this example, the consequence of having a fixed mindset—not going for it when you could've gotten a promotion—is clear.

After you have acknowledged your fixed mindset and identified its consequences, you can look at the potential benefits you could've gained if you had a growth mindset. The benefits that a growth mindset could've presented in the example above can be as follows: You would've believed in yourself and taken the necessary steps to get noticed at work, which may have landed you that promotion.

If you've been a prisoner of your fixed mindset for a long time, it may be difficult to truly identify the benefits you're missing out on. To help you identify benefits in your life, let's look at the four most common ones:

- Any obstacles or challenges you may face are seen as opportunities for you to learn and develop yourself.

- You believe that everything you do to develop yourself will help you gain long-term results.

- You see all feedback, regardless of how negative it may seem, as valuable insight and an opportunity to improve yourself.

- You don't see other people as competitors, but rather as mentors or advisors who can help you achieve the same level of success they have.

Always remember that mindsets are essentially a set of beliefs that can either keep you back or propel you toward the success you desire. Just like you can change your mind about something small, such as what you are eating for dinner, you can change your mindset when it comes to more significant decisions.

The Power of Yet

A powerful way to move from a fixed to a growth mindset is by learning to use the word "yet." This three-letter word is arguably one of the most powerful ones in the English language, as it releases you from any limitations you may struggle with and opens your mind to endless possibilities by turning a negative situation into a positive one filled with hope and opportunities.

Let's look at an example. Say you have a goal of adding exercise to your routine three times a week. You may decide to follow a specific eating plan to help you improve your lifestyle and bring you closer to your goal. When you refer to yourself or talk about the reason why you want to make this change, you may be tempted to use negative words, such as "I'm lazy" or "I haven't reached my goal weight." These ways of referring to yourself are all indications of a fixed mindset, as you not only see yourself in a negative way, but you aren't focusing on the possibilities of improving your life.

Now, if you simply add "yet" to many negative statements, you'll focus on the positives and the endless possibilities that wait in your future, signaling a growth mindset. Let's continue with the example above. If you say something like, "I haven't reached my goal weight yet," the sentence implies that you are not only capable of reaching your goal weight, but you are also going to get there.

By simply adding the word "yet" to your sentences, you can boost your self-esteem, increase your confidence, and start to take the leap to change your mindset from fixed to growth.

Self-Acceptance Is the Key

While you're introducing the word "yet" into your daily life, you should also work at accepting yourself, as this is commonly believed to be one of the keys to finding true happiness in your life. When you accept yourself for who you are, you won't judge your own self-worth based on what you have achieved but rather on who you are as a person. As a result, your self-esteem won't take a dive every time you make a mistake or struggle.

Self-acceptance is all about making peace with who you are, what you have achieved so far, and where you are currently in your life. Once you have accepted your true self, you can focus on working on your weaknesses or flaws without being critical of yourself. You can then actively work at improving and aligning yourself to reach your goals. When you do this, you will find yourself happier and acting with more confidence and enthusiasm while also being able to solve problems that may arise quicker.

Take some time to think about yourself and your life. What are your strengths and weaknesses? What are you really happy with? What aspects of your life do you struggle to make peace with? What flaws make you feel self-conscious about yourself? Delving deep into who you really are can be a difficult and emotional exercise. Be patient with yourself. If you ever feel overwhelmed by what you uncover, take a break, and go do something that relaxes you. It's important that you're in the right frame of mind when you do this type of soul-searching. However, as uncomfortable as this may be, try your best to return to it as soon as you're feeling ready.

Once you have a better idea of your flaws or other aspects of your life that you struggle with, you can start to work on accepting them. Remind yourself that nobody is perfect, but you should never allow your imperfections to prevent you from living your best life. Find a way to accept and love the things you can't change and make plans to actively work on the things you can change. Remember to use the word "yet" when you work on your plans for change.

When you accept your flaws, you gain complete power over these aspects of your life, and unwanted opinions or judgments from others won't affect you as badly as before. If you've accepted and embraced your imperfections, no one can shame you for having them, and you won't live your life believing that you aren't good enough.

What's more, when you accept your flaws, you'll also attract other people to your life who will be equally acceptable and may even appreciate you even more because of these imperfections. You'll create a healthy environment where you'll be able to excel in all aspects of your life.

Embracing Change

The more you work at accepting yourself and embracing your flaws, the happier you'll be and the easier you'll be able to adjust to change. It's inevitable that you'll face various changes in both your personal and professional lives. Fighting against these changes is a fruitless exercise that will only lead to frustration and unhappiness in your life. However, if you learn to embrace the changes in your life, you'll learn to see them as valuable opportunities to learn and develop. Embracing change is, therefore, essential for growth in your life, as it helps you to fine-tune many skills or abilities, such as:

- **Flexibility:** Change will help you become more flexible in life and take more unexpected things in stride. If you can learn to adapt easily to unplanned and unforeseen events, you will be able to stay calm no matter what happens and seek out the positives in them.

- **Innovation:** When you embrace change, you'll be able to think more innovatively, which may lead you to consider solutions to problems you might have never even thought of. If you're constantly afraid of making mistakes or how others may judge you, you won't give yourself the creative freedom and positive environment to think outside the box.

- **Awareness:** Change doesn't have to be scary. If you decide to embrace change, you'll remove a lot of the fear of the unknown that may have pushed you down in the past. Without this fear, you'll be able to focus not only on what your next step should be but also on how you're feeling with every step you do take. As a result, you'll be able to address any unwarranted negative emotions immediately.

Embracing change brings you more benefits than simply the three listed above. You will become a more evolved person who will be able to adapt to life's challenges a lot easier. You will be able to expand your horizons more than you ever thought would be possible, make better connections with other people who want the best for you, and take more calculated risks, which can increase your success even more.

While it may sound easy enough to simply say you should embrace change, this can be difficult, especially if you've been a prisoner of a fixed mindset for too long. However, if you start by taking these small steps, you can get there:

- **Practice self-care:** Have you ever heard the saying, "You can't pour from an empty cup?" If you don't make time to take care of yourself, you won't be able to do everything in your power to achieve your goals, and any small change that you may face can be extremely overwhelming. Always remember that taking some time to take care of yourself is never selfish; it's essential and should always be a priority. Take time to do things that you enjoy or that will help you relax, especially when you're under a lot of pressure.

- **Ignore our fight, flight, or freeze instinct:** When you experience high levels of stress or anxiety, the cortisol levels in your body will rise, resulting in you experiencing the fight, flight, or freeze instinct to help you deal with the situation. This natural defense mechanism will, however, mostly result in you going back to what you know instead of taking the risk of trying something new. Unless your life is in danger, try to ignore your stress instincts by doing something different.

- **You don't always need to have all the answers:** When you embrace change, you'll open yourself to many new experiences in life. This may come with the added stress of not having all the answers to solve problems you may encounter along the way. However, the more you do this, the more you'll realize that you don't need to have all the answers. You'll increase your confidence in your ability to solve problems as you go, and you will also realize that there are likely many people in your life that you can rely on to give you advice and guidance.

- **Constantly look at new perspectives:** While dealing with the uncertainties that may come with embracing change, you'll learn to look at your problems from new perspectives, which can open your way of thinking drastically. The more you look at your problems from new perspectives, the easier it will be not only to solve them but also to deal with the uncertainties that change may bring.

- **Live your dream:** You may have entered into a career when you were young, thinking this is all you can do or that it will provide you with a large enough income to live comfortably. However, as you get older, you may realize that there are many other things that you wish you could do. If you get comfortable with embracing change, you'll have less fear of following your dreams and may even find yourself taking the risk to do so. This doesn't have to mean giving up your current career; it can simply mean starting something on the side to bring more fulfillment to your life.

- **Celebrate the uncertainties:** When you plan your life to the T, remain in your comfort zone, and leave nothing to chance, you may find yourself getting bored more easily. However, if you learn to embrace change and celebrate the many uncertainties you may face. As scary as these may be, they will also bring some excitement to your life and make sure that it remains interesting.

Always remember that having a growth mindset isn't like drinking a potion that will magically improve your life. Instead, it will set you on a path where you're willing to do whatever you can to improve your life, help you identify what you can control, and assist you in determining what steps you can and should take to turn your dreams into a reality.

While this will lay the perfect foundation for you, you'll still need to put in the effort and take the steps to break free from your comfort zone and try new things. It will require hard work, but it will be extremely rewarding, and you will start reaping the benefits shortly after starting this process.

From Comfort to Growth

If you stay in your comfort zone, you will struggle to break free from the fixed mindset that may have been holding you back. However, if you try new things and step outside your comfort zone, you'll also be working on developing a mindset that will help you grow and excel. You will start to believe in yourself and your abilities more than ever before and put yourself on the path to reaching your dreams. The following steps can help you get outside your comfort zone:

- **Identify your comfort zone**: If you don't know what your comfort zone is and how far it stretches, you may not even realize that you're a prisoner of your own fear. This is why it's so important to identify your comfort zone. Think about the things you can do comfortably and without experiencing much stress. What can you do easily without giving it much thought? What do you do exceptionally well? Consider your personal and professional life, as you may have different comfort zones in the various aspects of your life. Once you have identified the various comfort zones you may have, choose two that you want to start working on first: One in your personal life and one in your professional life.

- **Find the edge of your comfort zone**: After you've identified what comfort zones you want to step out of first, determine how far they reach. Think about the tasks that you can do effortlessly in your comfort zone. At what point do you start to experience fear? This will help you find the limits, or outer edges, of your comfort zone. For example, if you prefer to have set routines in your life, you may get extremely frustrated if people or circumstances push you out of your routine. The moment you start getting frustrated is the edge of your comfort zone.

- **Make a list**: While staying within these two comfort zones, think about the tasks associated with them that you don't feel comfortable with. Are there things you would really like to be able to do but avoid out of fear? If you don't deeply want to be able to do something, let go of that task and continue your search until you find something that matters to you. If you don't deeply want to do something, you won't fully commit to stepping out of your comfort zone to achieve it.

- **What can you do now**: Look at your lists of things you would really like to do and identify one thing on each list that you will be able to do within the next week. Going over to action while you're feeling motivated to make changes to your life is a vital step in getting out of your comfort zone. I would suggest that you make sure this first item on your list is small, realistic, and achievable so that you will easily be able to complete it and boost your confidence. For example, if you want to change your lifestyle to introduce intermittent fasting, don't aim for a full-day fast right from the start. Simply see if you can eat your breakfast an hour later or cut sugar and milk out of your coffee. Once you've decided on your first step, add it to your schedule and do what you have to in order to complete it.

- **Evaluate your own response**: As you work on improving your life by taking the first small step out of your comfort zone, pay close attention to how you feel, why you feel that way, and how you react to these emotions. Deal with any negative emotions with understanding, without judgment, and celebrate the positive feelings you will experience once you've completed this step.

- **Do it again**: Once you're done with the first step, repeat this process to take the second step that will bring you closer to your goal.

- **Find a mentor or accountability buddy**: If you struggle with completing certain steps, think about someone in your life who can act as a mentor and advise you on what steps you can take next. There will likely be many people in your life who have achieved the type of success you desire and who will be willing to help you on your journey. If not, discuss your plans with someone you trust and keep them updated on the progress you make along the way. When you have someone who checks up on your progress and holds you accountable for your actions, you'll be more likely to push through the tough times to reach your desired success.

Self-Assessment: Building Self-Esteem

Now that you have a much better understanding of the impact a fixed mindset can have in your life and how taking small steps to move to a growth mindset can bring you closer to the success you desire, let's put this into practice. The following exercise was designed specifically to help you transition from your comfort zone to your growth zone by embracing change and improving your self-esteem (Byrne, 2020):

Identify your comfort zone in various aspects of your life: To do this, think about where you feel most comfortable and confident.

Work	Family	Friends	Children	Home
Hobbies or interests	Health	Asking for help	Other	Notes

Identify the outer edges of your comfort zones: This is where you're still comfortable doing something but will start to experience some fear.

Work	Family	Friends	Children	Home

Hobbies or interests	Health	Asking for help	Other	Notes

Make a list: Identify things that you really would like to do but don't feel comfortable doing yet.

Work	Family	Friends	Children	Home

Hobbies or interests	Health	Asking for help	Other	Notes

What can you do now? Pick one area from the above (or two if you want to work on your personal and professional comfort zones at the same time). It can be helpful to work on the thing that may be easiest for you to do so that you can gain confidence before you move on to more difficult tasks.

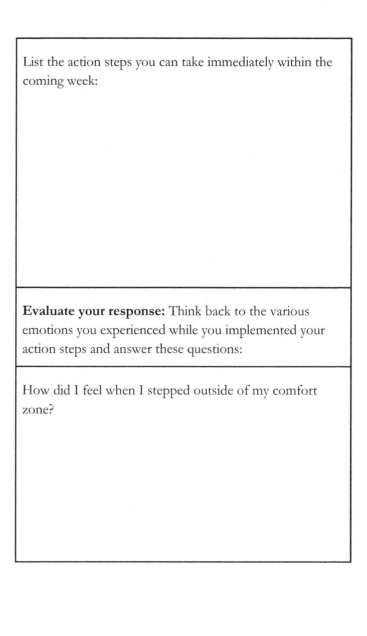

List the action steps you can take immediately within the coming week:

Evaluate your response: Think back to the various emotions you experienced while you implemented your action steps and answer these questions:

How did I feel when I stepped outside of my comfort zone?

What negative emotions or thoughts did I experience?

What can I do to overcome these negative emotions and thoughts?

What positive change did I experience?

> What can I do next to bring more positive change into my life?

Taking the first step toward a better, more positive you, where you embrace change and move from your comfort zone to your growth zone, is arguably one of the most important ones you can take. If you can do this effectively, it will set you up for more success and motivate you to make even more changes to get you closer to the success you desire. Remember, you might not be there yet, but you can get there.

Unfortunately, you may face many obstacles on your journey, which can bring unnecessary negativity into your life. In the next chapter, we'll address why so many people love misery and what you can do to overcome negative thoughts and emotions.

Chapter 3:

Why Do We Love Misery?

Believing in negative thoughts is the single greatest obstruction to success. –Charles F. Glassman

Having negative or limiting thoughts can not only affect your ability to reach your goals but can also impact your whole outlook on life. Let's look at the well-known example of two shoe salesmen who were sent from Britain to Africa to investigate the potential of branching out on this continent. The first salesman reported back that there was no potential in Africa, as nobody there wears shoes. The second salesman saw it completely differently. He reported that since nobody wears shoes, there is massive potential for gaining massive success on this continent.

Both salesmen investigated the exact same situation, but their reports provided the complete opposite advice. One saw it as a positive opportunity filled with many potential benefits, while the other found it to be only negative and saw problems and other disadvantages. It all came down to one salesman choosing to apply a growth mindset while the other was a victim of his negative, limiting beliefs.

Now, while keeping this story in mind, think about your own life. How often do you see the positive in situations you encounter? Or, are you often stuck viewing your situations from a negative perspective, identifying problems instead of opportunities? What benefits can you gain in your life if you're able to break free from your limiting beliefs and negative outlook?

To help you achieve this, we'll now look at simple strategies and techniques you can introduce into your life, starting with identifying and eliminating counter mindsets.

Identify Your Counter Mindset

We've discussed fixed and growth mindsets in some detail. Now, let's look at counter-mindsets and their impact on your life. Everything you do in life contributes to your mindset. If you succeed at a task, you'll have a positive mindset the next time you take on a similar task, as you'll know that you're capable of completing the task successfully. However, if you've failed at a specific task in the past, you'll be filled with negative thoughts, self-doubt, and limiting beliefs the next time you have to work on the same task. These mindsets that stop you from achieving the results you desire are called counter-mindsets.

Since they are specifically linked to past experiences, it can be difficult to break free from counter-mindsets. This is because they are fueled by automatic negative thoughts (ANTs), often without you even realizing it. You'll need to make a conscious effort to become more aware of these ANTs to see how often you have them and then deliberately change your thoughts to make them more positive. Be patient with yourself when you do this. Depending on the strength and severity of these ANTs, it may take a consistent effort over a long period of time to effectively break them. Think of your mindset like a muscle: The weaker it is, the more effort you need to put in to strengthen it, and even when it's strong, you need to continue practicing it, so you don't lose your strength.

Facing the ANTagonist

Since ANTs are often responsible for you having a counter-mindset, let's take a deeper look into why you have these thoughts. You may wonder why you're having negative thoughts in the first place. There are two reasons for this. First, these thoughts can protect you from danger. When your body perceives a threat, your cortisol levels will rise, resulting in your fight, flight, or freeze response. The thoughts you have at this moment are your brain's way of trying to protect you from this threat. Unfortunately, unless you've trained your mind effectively, it can result in these negative thoughts taking control of your life for much longer than they need to and after the perceived threat has already been removed from your life.

The second reason for your ANTs may be a result of your negative ways of thinking becoming a habit. When you start to think negatively about yourself, your abilities, your life, or your environment, you'll be more prone to negative thoughts, and the stronger your negative pathways in your brain become.

While it's completely normal and most people will have ANTs, it can change your brain's chemistry, resulting in many bad effects on your body:

- Your brain will produce fewer feel-good hormones and chemicals, such as serotonin and dopamine.

- Your brain's production of proteins needed for new cell formation will be slowed down.

- Your risk for mental illnesses as well as neurodegenerative diseases will increase.

Now that you understand some of the physical and mental consequences your ANTs may have in your life, it's important that you take some time to understand what major ANTs you have in your life that may negatively affect you. While some of your ANTs will be obvious, others may be more hidden. It may also be that you don't want to admit to having certain ANTs in your life, as you will have to step outside of your comfort zone to address them. However, if you want to improve your life and mindset, you need to break free from the shackles of these negative thoughts.

To help you identify some of the ANTs in your life, the following common ANTs may help direct your thinking to some of the negative thoughts you may often repeat:

- **Black-and-white thinking**: If you constantly use the words "always" or "never" in negative sentences, you may be guilty of black-and-white thinking. This can include sentences such as "I always get it wrong" or "I'm never going to solve this problem." With this, you are setting yourself up for failure, as your thoughts make it clear that you don't expect to ever succeed.

- **Focusing on the negatives**: This happens when you constantly and sometimes even unconsciously seek out the negatives in all situations and dismiss any good or positives there might be. In everything you do and that happens to you, you have the choice to either focus on the thorns in the rose bush or be grateful that the thorns are keeping the rose flowers safe from predators. It's up to you how you want to view it.

- **Fortune-telling**: This isn't someone looking at tarot cards or tea leaves that tell you what will happen in the future, but rather those who believe that the worst possible things will always happen to them. Due to their constant expectation of the worst, they will seek out the negatives, increasing the odds of this becoming a reality.

- **Mind reading**: This is when you believe that you always know what someone else is thinking, and most of the time, you'll assume that these thoughts are negative. You don't give them a chance to explain their thoughts, as you already think that you know what they're thinking.

- **Thinking with your feelings**: This happens when you never stop to question your negative thoughts or feelings but simply believe them to be the truth, whether there is any proof to justify these feelings or thoughts or not.

- **Being ruled by "shoulds:"** If you allow yourself to feel guilty about your actions—or lack thereof—you may struggle with this ANT. No matter what the situation is, you will look for reasons to make you feel guilty or like you haven't done enough.

- **Using labels**: Continuously using negative labels, such as "fat," "stupid," or "lazy," will likely result in you having this ANT. The more you use these types of labels, the more they will become self-fulfilling prophecies in that if you believe you're stupid, you will act stupid, or if you believe you're lazy, you will procrastinate your tasks so that you can appear to be lazy.

- **Taking things personally**: In life, there will be people who say things you don't like or treat you in a way you don't agree with. While you can't control the words and actions of others, you can control how you choose to react to them. If you have a habit of taking things personally and beating yourself up over the actions of others, you may be dealing with an ANT that's controlling your life.

- **Blaming others**: The last ANT has to do with not taking responsibility for your own actions but rather choosing to blame others for your struggles. While there may be times when others are responsible for what happens to you, you are ultimately accountable for your own life and should accept responsibility without finding someone to blame.

Being aware of the ANTs that may be present in your life will help you identify them whenever they occur so that you can choose to replace them with positive thoughts and actions. The more you practice challenging them, the less power they will have over your life. It's important to keep in mind that it may be difficult to manage and let go of your ANTs. However, if you take small steps to first check their validity, you'll be well on your way to eliminating them from your life.

Some steps can include:

- **Question yourself:** If you question yourself and your ANT every time you experience it, you will not only see that this thought isn't valid but also that there are more positive ways to look at your situations. Questions you may want to ask yourself include:

    ○ Is this thought based on the truth?

    ○ Does this thought help me move forward?

    ○ What are other possible ways of looking at my situation?

    ○ If one of my friends had this negative thought, what advice would I give them?

- **Write down your ANTs:** If you make notes of your ANTs as you experience them, you'll be able to identify a pattern or trigger of negativity in your life. Knowing what your triggers are will help you anticipate your negative thoughts and choose to react in different ways.

- **Give your inner critic a name:** If you can give your inner critic a name or even attach an imaginary image to personify them, you can help reduce the impact your ANTs have on your life. This is because by naming your inner critic, it will be like someone else is saying the harsh words, and you are not thinking of them. As simple as this technique sounds, it can help keep you from owning your thoughts, and, similar to how you don't have to listen to the opinions of people you don't know, you don't have to believe or respond to your inner critics' opinions.

- **Create positive replacement thoughts:** As you become aware of the triggers of your ANTs, it can be helpful to write them down and include a positive replacement thought on your list. This will not only give you time to think about how you'd like to react or think but also help you become more aware of the triggers for your ANTs, for example:

  - **Trigger:** I made a mistake at work.

  - **ANT:** I am useless and a complete failure. I will probably get fired soon.

  - **Positive thought:** Everyone makes mistakes. How can I learn from this and turn my mistake into an opportunity to improve?

- **Change my "shoulds" and "shouldn'ts":** When you use statements with these words in them, you are creating the impression that you don't want to do something but must force yourself to do it. For example, if you're assigned a big project at work, you may tell yourself something, such as, "I should start working on it" or "I shouldn't procrastinate." This creates the impression that you don't actually want to work on this project but that you have to. Instead, if you tell yourself something like, "I want to get started on the project" or "I love how I feel every time I complete a section of the project," you will feel more comfortable with your ability to get the work done.

- **Meditate:** Meditation can help you to relax when you're struggling with your ANTs, as it can quiet your mind so that you can accept your thoughts without judgment, understand that your ANTs are only thoughts, not the truth and that you can move past them. Deep breathing techniques or practicing yoga can have similar effects on your mind.

- **Practice gratitude:** No matter how negative your thoughts may feel, there are always positives in your life. If you create a habit of practicing gratitude by naming at least one thing you're grateful for every day, you'll force yourself to seek out the good in your life, and as a result, your brain will release more feel-good hormones and chemicals, such as dopamine, serotonin, and oxytocin.

Challenging Your Negative Thoughts

While we've briefly discussed some questions you can ask yourself to question the validity of your ANTs, you can take it even further by including positive thoughts or answers to some questions that can help you challenge your negative thoughts:

- **Possible ANT:** John didn't greet me when I walked past him today. I've clearly made him angry.

  - **Question:** Am I having a negative thought or reacting to fear?

  - **Explanation:** While the thought may seem real, you may just be reacting to a fear you have. Make sure you're reacting to facts, not fears.

  - **Positive replacement:** If I had made John angry, he would've discussed this with me. I can't think of anything I've done, so John probably didn't see me.

- **Possible ANT:** My boss didn't assign me to work on the project. I am terrible at my work.

  ○ **Question:** Am I jumping to conclusions?

  ○ **Explanation:** You may react to a situation based on what you believe is the truth without finding out what the case really is. Always seek out the facts before you simply react.

  ○ **Positive replacement:** I have a lot of other work on my plate, and that is most likely the reason why my boss didn't want me to work on the new project.

- **Possible ANT:** I'll never be able to find the right answer.

  ○ **Question:** What alternatives are there?

  ○ **Explanation:** There may be many other possible viewpoints, not just the negative ones you're thinking about.

  ○ **Positive replacement:** There are many different possibilities that I haven't considered yet. What other alternatives have I overlooked?

- **Possible ANT:** I'll never be good enough.

- Question: What are the consequences of my thinking?

- Explanation: All your thoughts will have consequences, whether positive or negative. If you allow your ANTs to run free in your mind, they may keep you from achieving the success you desire.

- Positive replacement: There are many things that I'm excellent at and some things that I still need to work on. It's up to me to learn what I can to improve at these things.

- **Possible ANT:** I can't even think of basic answers to questions.

  - Question: Am I asking the right questions?

  - Explanation: There may be times that you ask questions that don't really have answers.

  - Positive replacement: Some questions just don't have answers, no matter how much I try. There's no point in looking for answers if they don't exist.

- **Possible ANT:** It's not even possible to do worse than I did. I should simply give up.

- ○ **Question:** Are all my thoughts all-or-nothing type?

- ○ **Explanation:** Nothing is ever all good or all bad. It's important to remember that, regardless of how bad the situation may seem, there will always be some good that you should consider.

- ○ **Positive replacement:** I may not have done as well as I wanted to, but I did my best, and that is good enough.

- **Possible ANT:** I always fail at everything I do.

  - ○ **Question:** How often do I use ultimatum type of words?

  - ○ **Explanation:** Again, you might make mistakes along the way, but the chances are good that if you really think about your life, you'll remember many times that you achieved amazing success. Try to avoid using words such as "always," "never," "everyone," "everything," and "nothing."

  - ○ **Positive replacement:** I am capable of many great things, and one error won't define my life. I won't judge my entire being based on a single event.

- **Possible ANT:** I'm bound to be alone now that my best friend has moved away.

  - **Question:** Am I focusing only on my weaknesses?

  - **Explanation:** If you've had a long relationship or friendship with someone, you may tie a lot of your self-worth and identity to them. However, it's important that you remember that you are your own person and shouldn't define yourself by any connections you may have with other people.

  - **Positive replacement:** As much as I value my relationships with other people, I'm capable of creating new friendships.

- **Possible ANT:** I must be incredibly stupid for making this mistake.

  - **Question:** Was the mistake I made really my fault?

  - **Explanation:** While you may be to blame for some of the mistakes you make, others aren't within your control, and you shouldn't accept any blame for them.

- Positive replacement: I will only blame myself for mistakes that I know for a fact are my fault.

- **Possible ANT:** My boss hates me. There's no other explanation for the way they shouted at me.

  - **Question:** Am I taking things that have nothing to do with me too personally?

  - **Explanation:** You aren't responsible for the reactions of other people. While their actions may have been directed toward you in a negative way, you shouldn't have to accept responsibility for it.

  - **Positive replacement:** There may be something else that's bothering my boss that could've made them react in that way. I won't take their overreaction personally.

- **Possible ANT:** My actions aren't good enough. I'm not working through my to-do list.

  - **Question:** Am I trying to be perfect?

  - **Explanation:** Even with the best intentions, there may be days that you simply can't complete all the tasks you set out to do. This is why you should always make sure that the tasks on your list are realistic and easily achievable. Also, remind yourself that it's impossible to be perfect. Instead, do your best and learn to accept your imperfections.

- ○ **Positive replacement:** My best is always good enough. I should strive to do my best instead of wanting to be perfect.

- **Possible ANT:** This is never going to work.

  - ○ **Question:** Am I expecting disaster to strike?

  - ○ **Explanation:** Sometimes it may be difficult to foresee a positive outcome when everything seems to be doom and gloom. However, just because a negative outcome might seem to be the most likely result, it may not be as bad as you expect. Actively seek out the positives.

  - ○ **Positive replacement:** Although this may seem bad, it doesn't have to be like that. I will look for the positives.

- **Possible ANT:** I made such a fool of myself today. I will never be able to face those people again.

○ **Question:** Am I putting too much importance on certain events?

○ **Explanation:** While some situations may be extremely embarrassing at times, are they really that important? Will you still feel embarrassed in a month or even a year? If not, don't let this affect you too much. You can overcome it.

○ **Positive replacement:** I felt quite embarrassed, but I won't let this impact my life.

• **Possible ANT:** There's no point in trying. I won't get this right.

○ **Question:** What can I do to change my situation?

○ **Explanation:** Sometimes your situation may look bleak. However, there are always things you can do to improve your circumstances. You may just have to actively search for them.

○ **Positive replacement:** I won't just back down and accept things. I'll focus on what I can change and forget about the things I can't control.

Overcome Your Limiting Belief

Once you're done working on your ANTs, let's focus on any limiting beliefs you may have. Limiting beliefs are ungrounded or false beliefs that keep you from working toward reaching your goals. Similar to ANTs, they can make you feel like you're not good enough to achieve your desired outcomes, so there's no point in even trying to pursue the success you desire. It can even stop you from trying something new, such as a different flavor of ice cream or a combination of foods.

While many of your limiting beliefs will have a negative effect on your life, it's important to understand that some may even be positive. An example of this is believing that stealing is wrong. This belief will help you set a boundary that will stop you from taking something that doesn't belong to you. Or it can keep you from shouting at the top of your lungs while you're in public or at a place where it will be deemed inappropriate.

However, not all limiting beliefs help you keep your behavior intact. As we've said, some can keep you from pursuing your goals and reaching the success you desire, often without you even realizing it. While you may have many different limiting beliefs, the three most common types are:

- You feel like you're unable to do something because there's something wrong with you.

- You feel like you can't achieve your goals because other people will stand in your way.

- You feel like it's pointless to try to reach your version of success because the tasks you need to complete are simply too difficult.

Think about the limiting beliefs you may have in your life. Write them down as you think about them; this will help you when you start to work through them. If you are struggling to identify them, the following common ones may help steer you in the right direction:

Limiting Beliefs About Yourself

As we've mentioned, some of your limiting beliefs will be deeply rooted in yourself and your personality:

- **Age:** You might believe that you're too old to make drastic changes to your life—career and relationships—and, therefore, remain stuck in circumstances that aren't good for you or won't bring you closer to your goal. Alternatively, you may believe that you're too young to make certain decisions, such as getting married or going after a big promotion at work. Once you truly think about it, you'll realize that people use the exact same excuse—their age—to make changes to the exact same aspects of their lives. Ultimately, you're never too young or too old to make changes that will benefit you.

- **Personal traits:** There may be specific things about your personality or life that are holding you back, such as thinking you're too dumb to apply for a scholarship or specific job, too ugly to talk to the person you're really attracted to, or that you're too overweight to join the gym to improve your health. While there may not always be a lot we can do to change these traits, it's important that you change how you think about yourself and see them. Once you realize that, even though you may be short, it shouldn't keep you from playing basketball, you'll understand that you're actually capable of anything you put your mind to. You simply have to believe in yourself and your own abilities.

- **Emotions:** Your feelings can often result in you having to limit beliefs, which may have a massive impact on your ability to move forward and aim for the success you desire. How many times have you felt too embarrassed by an event in your past to go to certain places? Or do you think that because you're suffering from depression, no one will like you? Unfortunately, the thing that you're avoiding most in your life might just be the thing that you need to do to overcome the limiting beliefs that are holding you back. Let's take depression as an example: If you're constantly feeling sad, isolating yourself from others will simply increase your sadness. While spending time with others isn't a magical cure for your mental health problems, it can help improve your mood and reduce your feelings of sadness.

Limiting Beliefs About the World

Some of the limiting beliefs you may have will be based on the world you live in:

- **Disapproval:** You might think that people will judge you, disapprove of your decisions, disrespect you, or accept you for who you truly are. Think about how often you base your decisions on what other people will think. When this is the case, you're fighting a losing battle as you're prioritizing the opinions of others over your own happiness and success. The reality is that people don't care about others nearly as much as you might think, and if others don't approve of your choices, will that really have an impact on your life? You're the only one who is living your life and has to live with the decisions you make, so always do what's best for you, not other people.

- **Prejudice:** Unfortunately, there will always be people who discriminate against others simply based on race, gender, age, cultural background, religious beliefs, or even body type or build. As much as this is extremely unfair, it is a reality that many people have to live with on a daily basis. However, you shouldn't hesitate to go for your goals out of fear of being discriminated against. Let's take racism as an example: While there are many racists in this world, you shouldn't assume that the people you need to assist you in reaching your goals will judge you based on the color of your skin. Believe in yourself, your capabilities, and show the racists that you won't back down.

- **Being special:** In some limiting beliefs, you may feel like you can't achieve the success you desire due to others' inability to understand you and your talents. You may feel that your out-of-the-box thinking will be too eccentric for others or that your sense of humor might be so dry or sarcastic that others won't get you. While you may believe that you're extremely special, others might not agree, and your sense of entitlement can result in them seeing you as arrogant. Make sure that you remain humble at all times, and while you may have special talents that set you apart from others, you shouldn't let this make you feel boastful.

Limiting Beliefs About Life

Some of your limiting beliefs might be about life in general, or more specifically, your beliefs about what a normal life may look like:

- **Missed the boat**: You might believe that you're too late to do what you really want to do. You may feel like other people have already had your great idea or achieved what you desire. You may feel like there isn't enough success left for you, so you use this as an excuse not to take the risk to improve your life. However, once you realize that there is more than enough success going around for you to get help, you'll understand that you shouldn't and can't let this limiting belief keep you from doing what you deeply want.

- **Time**: Many people believe that they don't have enough time to make the changes they need or do what they can to achieve the success they desire. Think about your own life. How often do you feel like you don't have enough time to do what's important to you? This can be making changes to your lifestyle to improve your health or completing an important project at work that will win you good graces with your superiors. You're choosing the safe and comfortable option instead of stepping over into your growth zone, where you'll realize that you're capable of anything.

- **It doesn't exist**: You may struggle to differentiate between what exists and what doesn't, leaving you stuck in your own world of feeling confused over what your next step may be. For example, you may believe that success is nothing other than a myth that people have created to push others to do more work or that humans are inherently selfish and there's nothing you can do to make them care for others. These can be difficult beliefs to manage and overcome, as you might not always be aware of them or the effect they can have on your life. Think about what is stopping you from trying to improve your life. While these won't necessarily appear to be limiting beliefs, they're still stopping you from going after your dreams.

Now that you're forming a better understanding of the limiting beliefs you may have, you may wonder what you can do to overcome them. While we've discussed some tips on how you can deal with the various limiting beliefs you may have in your life, the following four questions can be very helpful in testing the validity of your beliefs and pinpoint what you can do to change them or reduce the effect they may have on your life:

- What proof do I have that my belief is real?

- What impact does this belief have?

- What alternative beliefs can I create to reduce the impact of this belief?

- How can I test my chosen alternative beliefs to make sure they are true before I implement them?

Self-Assessment

Let's take the next step in overcoming your limiting beliefs by doing a self-assessment test. Read through each statement in the table below and ask yourself how true it is in your life on a scale from 0 to 5, with 0 being not true at all and 5 being true most of the time. You can either circle or highlight your answer on the table below or write your answer on a sheet of paper (Goodman, n.d.):

I'll never achieve what I want in life.	0	1	2	3	4	5
I'm not capable of changing the things about myself I don't like.	0	1	2	3	4	5
I need others to achieve success.	0	1	2	3	4	5
I can't change my circumstances.	0	1	2	3	4	5
I deserve what I have in life.	0	1	2	3	4	5
I'm mostly unhappy with my life.	0	1	2	3	4	5
I'll always have some limitations in my life.	0	1	2	3	4	5
I can't do the things I actually want to do.	0	1	2	3	4	5

I give up when things get too difficult.	0	1	2	3	4	5
I don't have the resources to reach my goals.	0	1	2	3	4	5
I'm unable to make big changes in my life.	0	1	2	3	4	5
My financial situation will never improve.	0	1	2	3	4	5
Even if I try everything, I won't be able to do what I want.	0	1	2	3	4	5
My romantic relationship doesn't fulfill my needs.	0	1	2	3	4	5
I feel stuck where I am in my life.	0	1	2	3	4	5

I can't change other people.	0	1	2	3	4	5
There's a limited amount of love in life.	0	1	2	3	4	5
Things are what they are, and there's nothing I can do to change them.	0	1	2	3	4	5
My future will be exactly the way my life is at the moment.	0	1	2	3	4	5

Once you've worked through the test, calculate your answers to understand the impact your limiting beliefs may have on your life:

- **0 to 40**: You're living a life fairly free from limiting beliefs and have a good grip on reality and your own abilities. There may be some beliefs that are still holding you back, but if you work on actively improving your life, you can overcome the small things that may still be holding you back. Consider replacing these with beliefs that will empower you.

- **41 to 60**: You have some limiting beliefs in certain parts of your life. Since they only affect some aspects of your life, you can still achieve great success. Think about the limiting beliefs you do have in your life. Once you've identified them, consider which ones you want to work on first and decide what alternatives you can use to reduce the impact of your beliefs.

- **61 to 80**: You have significant beliefs that are impacting various aspects of your life. Try your best to identify as many of them as possible and do what you can to work on them one at a time. If you try to work on too many at once, you may find yourself easily overwhelmed. By taking one belief at a time, you'll be able to hone your focus on that one before you address the next one.

- **81 to 100**: Your beliefs have a massive impact on your life and your ability to achieve any form of success. You may feel stuck and like you don't have it in you to make big enough changes to reach your goals. This is the first limiting belief you need to change. Ask yourself what proof there is to validate this belief. Then, tell yourself repeatedly that you can make any changes you need in your life and that you can reach your goals. Look at your limiting beliefs and try to group them according to which ones are based on assumptions you've made, which ones are based on conclusions, and which ones were taught to you by others.

Understanding the ANTs and other negative beliefs you may have in your life is a massive first step in improving your life and reaching the success you desire. With every step you take to reduce the impact they have on your life; you'll also make strides in improving your mindset.

While you're making these changes, it's important that you're aware of any criticism you may have toward yourself and know when to set healthy boundaries. In the next chapter, we'll discuss this in more detail and give you tips on how you can flip the switch.

Chapter 4:

How Do You Flip the

Switch?

Remember, you have been criticizing yourself for years and it hasn't worked. Try approving yourself and see what happens. –
Louise L. Hay

While you're working through your limiting beliefs and other ANTs, you may come across other difficulties that you need to address sooner rather than later. This can include being too critical of yourself, which often stems from being a perfectionist.

This is what happened to Jane, a 28-year-old who had to learn to work through her self-criticism to become a happier person. All her life, she had extremely high expectations for herself. This made her struggle in many aspects of her life, including her academics at school, her work life, her personality, and her appearance. No matter what she did, she was never happy with how she looked; she constantly compared herself to other people who she considered to be "prettier" and often struggled to accept the person she saw in her mirror. She struggled with depression and social anxiety, which eventually led to her developing an eating disorder.

As part of her treatment, Jane had to attend cognitive-behavioral therapy. This wasn't a quick or easy fix. She attended numerous therapy sessions to change her way of thinking. Eventually, Jane realized how mean her inner critic can be, and she learned to ignore the voice of her inner critic to the point where she was able to soften and even mute it. She learned to move past the negative thoughts and limiting beliefs that have been holding her back for far too long and found herself in a place where she has made peace with herself, her thoughts, and her actions. She even grew to a place where she found self-love again.

Jane learned to let go of her self-criticism, calm her inner critic, and find peace in aspects of her life she never thought would be possible. You can also learn not to be so hard on yourself and when to let go. Truly understanding this can bring amazing calmness into your life, which will go a long way in decreasing your inner critic.

Stop Being Too Self-Critical

When you're overly critical of yourself, you'll constantly judge yourself and have extremely negative opinions of yourself. Self-criticism often stems from early childhood and can be the result of having strict parents or teachers, struggling with peer pressure at school, or being too competitive in sports. Apart from these childhood causes, self-criticism can also be a learned behavior when you are extremely strict with yourself and do not believe your actions are ever good enough. Some level of self-criticism can help you acknowledge and avoid mistakes, but it can also have damaging effects.

It's important to realize that your self-criticism isn't a part of your personality and that you shouldn't attach your self-worth to the opinions of your inner critic or allow them to affect the way you treat yourself. If you keep criticizing yourself in that way, particularly when there's no valid reason for your critique, your mental well-being will suffer, and you'll struggle even more to reach your goals. Some of the common consequences of self-criticism on your mental health can include:

- **Your relationships**: When you are overly critical of yourself, you'll struggle to build proper relationships with other people, as you'll constantly be filled with negative thoughts, words, and actions. This can keep you from making deep connections with other people and can result in you isolating yourself from other people. This loneliness can have an extremely negative impact on your mental health.

- **Eating disorders**: When your self-esteem suffers due to self-criticism, you'll find more faults with your appearance, which can lead to unhealthy eating habits. This results in either overeating to try to make you feel better or undereating in the hopes of improving your appearance. Eating disorders can affect not only your physical health but also your mental health.

- **Overwhelming feelings of guilt**: When you feel like you're constantly failing at something, you may feel extremely guilty for failing not only yourself but also the people affected by your decisions or actions. The more you allow these guilty feelings to take over your mind, the more you'll struggle to overcome them and be able to improve yourself.

- **Keeps you from self-improvement**: Struggling with self-criticism will keep you from focusing on yourself and doing what you can to better your life. This can hamper your personal growth, decreasing your self-esteem even more.

If you're currently overly critical of yourself, you don't need to feel hopeless about ever improving your life. You can take small steps to be kinder to yourself. While this may not bring success overnight, the continuous effort will have positive results. Steps you can take to overcome your self-criticism include:

- Make a list of your strengths and think of ways you can use them to do more things you're passionate about.

- If you've experienced any form of trauma, consider seeking help from a therapist.

- Think about what advice you'd give a friend in the same situation and follow your own advice.

- Forgive yourself when you do anything wrong and understand that you're only human.

- Always be mindful of what you're thinking, feeling, and choose how you want to react.

- Keep a journal of your emotions, daily actions, and look out for any patterns that can help you avoid negativity.

- Practice gratitude.

Another step you can take to reduce your self-criticism is to work on improving the way you view yourself. Your self-image develops over time and is influenced by many different external factors, such as your parents, teachers, peers, and the media. They affect how you view your personal strengths and weaknesses, which you, in turn, mirror back to your life. Everything you do and experience adds to this mirror and affects the way you see yourself in three ways:

- physical appearance (how you look)

- performance (how you're doing)

- relationships (how important you are)

It's important to remember that the image that's reflected in your mirror may be highly distorted from reality, either in a positive or negative way. You can have a highly inflated self-image where you focus predominantly on your strengths and may even believe your capabilities are superior. This can lead you to attempt things that are way beyond your means, which can increase your risk of failure. On the flip side, your self-image may be greatly lacking, resulting in you focusing mainly on your weaknesses, not realizing your own worth, and not being willing to try anything new due to your belief that you won't succeed.

Regardless of your current self-image, you can work on improving it, which will increase your satisfaction in life. You can learn to get a more realistic view of yourself by taking the following steps:

- Think about how you're currently seeing yourself and write down some keywords. These will help you determine what aspects you should work on.

- Make a list of your positive qualities or strengths. It can be helpful to ask people you trust to also list some of the strengths they see in you, as their view of your abilities will likely be different from yours.

- Identify strengths you may have forgotten you have or didn't realize were important in your life.

- Think about the labels you had to deal with as a child and consider what impact they may still have on your life.

- How often do you compare yourself to others? Think of specific instances where your self-image may be distorted as a result of making these comparisons.

- What can you do to develop your strengths? How can you turn your weaknesses into strengths?

- What positive affirmations can you introduce into your life to help you love yourself again and realize your self-worth?

- Constantly remind yourself that you are unique, capable of greatness, and have achieved many successes in the past.

While your self-image will often focus more on your capabilities, you also need to pay attention to your body image. This is directly linked to your physical appearance and your perception of your attributes. Your body image can directly affect your mental health: If you see your body in a positive light, you'll feel good about yourself, but if your body image is negative, you'll be more prone to low self-esteem, anxiety disorders, and even depression. You can work on improving your body image and accepting your physical appearance and imperfections. The following steps can help you in this process:

- Think about how you currently view your body. What do you consider to be your strengths, and what are your weaknesses?

- Are there any distortions between what you perceive your body to look like and reality?

- What assumptions do you have about the perfect body? Are they realistic? How much have you allowed the media to influence your view of the perfect body?

- What can you do to accept yourself and become comfortable with your body?

- What positive affirmations can you introduce into your life to improve your body image?

Befriending Your Inner Critic

While you're working on reducing your self-criticism, you'll find yourself dealing with your inner critic a lot. This is the little voice in your head that's expressing your criticism of yourself. It's important that you work on muting your inner critic and reducing the impact its words will have on your life.

In the previous chapter, we discussed personifying your inner critic by giving it a name and even attaching a caricature to it. This can be a great tool to regain control over your thoughts and emotions.

Another way of tackling your inner critic is by practicing self-compassion. If you allow your inner critic to reign free, it can result in you constantly feeling anxious and focusing only on the negatives, as if you're using a magnifying glass. It can cause you to become paranoid and question other people's motives, whether justified or not.

By practicing self-compassion exercises, you can decrease these negative effects in your life. One way of doing this is by treating yourself just like you would your best friend and making sure you use the same tone of voice and words you would comfort yourself. Become more aware of how you talk to yourself and compare this to what you're currently doing. The chances are good that you'll be shocked by this discovery and realize how harsh and unfair you can be toward yourself.

Another way of doing this is by becoming more mindful of staying in the present through meditation. When you're mindful, you focus only on what is currently happening and accept any thoughts and worries you may have without judgment. While there are many different meditation techniques you can practice, let's look at a simple one to start with:

- Sit in a comfortable, quiet place, either on a chair, on your bed, or on the floor. If you're sitting on something, make sure your feet are comfortably on the ground, and place your hands on your lap. As you become more accustomed to meditating, you'll be able to do this in any position or environment, but when you start with this, it's best to choose a place where you won't be interrupted.

- While sitting in this position, try to keep your back as straight as you possibly can, but don't focus too much on your posture. If it will help you, place a pillow behind your back to keep your back straight.

- Close your eyes and do a deep breathing exercise to calm yourself. Any breathing exercise will work as long as it helps you relax. Box breathing is very effective in this: Inhale through your nose for five seconds, hold your breath for five seconds, exhale through your mouth for five seconds, and hold your breath for five seconds.

- Focus only on your breathing as you set into a rhythm and feel how your lungs expand with every breath you take.

- If you have any thoughts, don't spend too much time thinking about them. Instead, accept them without judging yourself and turn your focus back to your breathing.

- Once you've settled into a good rhythm, you can do a quick body scan. Start with your feet, ankles, and calves by contracting and relaxing your muscles. Continue focusing on different parts of your body and how your body feels as you contract and relax your muscles.

- After you've completed your body scan, go back to focusing only on your breathing for a few cycles before you end your session. If you want, do a few stretches as you get up.

Two of the Three Deadly P's

Now that we've worked on your self-criticism and inner critic; let's look at other aspects that can make it difficult to focus on your tasks. These are often referred to as the three deadly Ps: perfectionism, procrastination, and people-pleasing. We'll discuss procrastination more in the next chapter, so let's focus now on beating your perfectionism and people-pleasing.

When you're a perfectionist, you'll constantly look for faults in everything that you do and never feel fully satisfied with what you're doing. You'll continuously look for different methods to try, and you'll beat yourself up when these still don't bring you the desired results. While some people will use their perfectionism as a motivational tool to improve themselves, or for others, it can bring a lot of anxiety, anger, depression, and even obsessive compulsions, which aren't good for their physical, emotional, or mental wellness. Your impossibly high standards can overwhelm you to such a degree that they can become completely debilitating, affecting not only your ability to complete tasks but also your relationships and quality of life. Common symptoms of perfectionism include:

- Feeling like you're failing at everything you do.

- Having difficulty relaxing or explaining to others what you're experiencing.

- Wanting to control everything and everyone around you.

- Obsessing overrules and whether others are following these rules.

- Procrastinating your tasks until you find the perfect way of doing them.

While your perfectionism may impact your life in many different ways, the most common ones include:

- **It gives you false motivation:** When you believe that whatever you're attempting isn't good enough, you may push yourself harder in an attempt to reach your perfect results. However, when you don't get there, your inner critic goes into overdrive, making you feel even worse about yourself than ever before. The reality is that nothing is ever perfect, and as much as you try to achieve this, you'll always find more things that you're unhappy about. This is why it's so important that you understand that not only is there no such thing as perfection, but also that your best is always good enough.

- **It takes your creativity:** Your drive to deliver tasks perfectly can reduce your ability to think outside the box, as you'll set your aim too high in an attempt to meet unrealistic standards. This can result in your perfectionism killing your dreams. When you set goals for yourself, always make sure they are realistic.

- **It makes receiving feedback more difficult:** When you aim for perfection, it can be difficult to receive and accept negative feedback, regardless of how constructive it may actually be. This can result in you feeling completely broken by anything that may be perceived as negative. Unfortunately, no matter how much you try, it's impossible to please everyone, which is why it's vital to not only understand the intention behind negative feedback but also to decide what you can use to improve yourself while discarding or even just accepting the rest.

- **It can cause burnout:** When you're constantly striving to achieve perfect results, you'll push yourself far beyond your limits in an effort to achieve your desired results. Not only will you try to work harder, but you'll also double and even triple-check your work to make sure it's as close to perfection as possible. This will put even more pressure on you, as you'll find things to second-guess and redo. Eventually, you'll find yourself so exhausted that you'll be unable to concentrate on your tasks, opening the door to mistakes. You need to understand where to draw the line between acceptable results and going beyond your limitations.

- **It takes your happiness:** Focusing on trying to get things done perfectly will keep you from enjoying and valuing the smaller things in life. What's more, you'll lack the flexibility you need to adjust to life's curveballs, making it even more difficult for you to find happiness regardless of your circumstances. If you can let go of your deep desire to achieve perfection, you'll be able to celebrate the smaller things in life and turn more negative situations into positives.

The second P we'll discuss now is people pleasing. While this may not sound like such a bad thing and may even be seen as caring for others, it can be when you sacrifice your own happiness for that of someone else. You'll put your own needs and wants aside to try to fulfill those of others, and you'll be highly influenced by their opinions. You may even agree with others simply to avoid conflict, whether this is in your own best interest or not. This again can result in you taking on too much, as you'll find it very difficult to say "no" to others, increasing your risk of burning yourself out.

To break your habit of people-pleasing, you need to be courageous, as you'll have to stand strong in who you are and stand up for what you believe. You'll also need courage to potentially disappoint others and deal with any backlash that may come with that. Let's look at other ways your people-pleasing may negatively affect you:

- **It creates mental blocks:** When you're so focused on making other people happy, you may lose sight of what's really important and what you need to do to achieve your goals. This can result in you being unmotivated, putting you in a slump where you'll struggle to complete even the simplest of tasks.

- **It makes you appear disingenuous:** If you focus too much on pleasing others, you may do things that are out of character or not aligned with your goals. This can create the impression that you're not being authentic. They may even lose faith in you. When people have this idea of you, it can be even more difficult for you to please them, resulting in you having to put even more effort into it and taking you even further away from your goals.

- **You may lose your identity:** Adding on to the previous point, when you're focused on pleasing others for too long, you may lose sight of who you are as a person and forget what is really important to you. This can result in your self-esteem taking a dive, as you'll be filled with self-doubt over what your next step should be.

Setting Healthy Boundaries

Setting healthy boundaries is a very effective way of not only dealing with your inner critic but also reducing your people-pleasing behavior and perfectionism. When you set a boundary, you're essentially telling yourself how far you're willing to go and what you decide is unacceptable. Furthermore, your boundaries will also help you to improve your self-esteem, as you'll define what treatment you're willing to accept and give you the freedom to know that you have a safe space in which you can live and thrive. Boundaries will even give you the opportunity to take back control over certain situations and accept responsibility for your own life and actions without judging yourself or risking pushing yourself too far.

Even though having boundaries holds many benefits in your life, many people don't know how to set them, communicate them to others, enforce them, or deal with situations where people overstep their boundaries. This can be because many people believe that announcing and enforcing your boundaries is a sign of arrogance when it is actually a sign of you standing up for yourself and what you believe in. Setting healthy boundaries is never selfish; it's an absolute necessity if you want to achieve a growth mindset.

Think about the boundaries you may need to set in your life. What are the aspects where you feel people may be taking advantage of you? What areas of your life do you want more control over? Where will you benefit from having a strict boundary to protect you? If, after answering these questions, you still feel unsure of what boundaries to consider setting in your life, the three most common boundaries include:

- **Mental:** This has to do with protecting your thoughts, opinions, beliefs, values, wants, and needs. These boundaries will help you stand firm in what you believe is right and in what opposing opinions you will allow in your life. It will also prevent your inner critic from overstepping your boundaries and, as a result, reduce the amount of self-criticism you need to deal with.

- **Physical:** This has to do with your body and your personal space. How close will you allow other people to come to you physically? What physical contact do you approve of? Also, consider what sexual boundaries you may need to set in your life.

- **Emotional:** This type of boundary is there to protect your feelings and choices. It shows that you respect yourself and demand that others respect you in the same way. This doesn't mean that you can use boundaries to excuse unreasonable emotional outbursts, but rather that you protect yourself, not only from others but also from yourself.

Boundaries are very personal, and no one has the right to tell you that your boundaries are wrong. They are there to protect you and give you the sense of safety you need to improve your life. However, you need to make sure that your boundaries are reasonable, as it can be helpful to get buy-in and understanding from the people who need to respect your limitations.

One way of ensuring your boundaries are reasonable is by measuring the emotional discomfort you experience when you think not only about the boundary and how you will feel when you set it but also how you will feel if someone doesn't respect it. The more emotional discomfort you experience, the more you'll know that this boundary is important enough for you to set.

Once you've decided on your boundaries, it's important to communicate them to everyone involved so that they are aware of what your limits are and what you won't tolerate anymore. In the beginning, you might find that people will overstep some of your boundaries as they are not used to your new rules. When this happens, gently remind them of your limits and that you can't tolerate that type of behavior going forward. Should this happen again, you'll have to decide how you will react. This can include distancing yourself from that person or adjusting your boundaries. How you deal with this is up to you and will depend on the importance of your boundary and the implications of it not being adhered to.

Self-Assessment: The Seven Critics

While you're busy introducing boundaries to your life, let's turn our attention back to your inner critic and examine what type of critic you have living inside of you. The following self-assessment questionnaire will not only discuss the seven types of critics there are but also give you insights into how you critique yourself.

Read through the following questions and score each one as follows:

- 4: Always

- 3: Frequently

- 2: Occasionally

- 1: Not often

- 0: Never

		Score
1.	I feel like I have many flaws.	
2.	I have very high standards for myself.	
3.	I hate it when I don't have control over something.	
4.	I push myself to do whatever I can to reach my goals.	
5.	I often give up before I even begin when I need to try something new.	
6.	There are many things about myself that I'm ashamed of.	
7.	I struggle to forgive myself for something I've done.	
8.	I know who I want to be and find it difficult to accept that I'm not there yet.	

9.	I struggle to control my impulsive behavior.	
10.	My self-confidence is so low that I doubt myself and my abilities.	
11.	I'm hard on myself when I make errors.	
12.	I find it difficult to remain positive about myself.	
13.	It's hard for me to go against how I was brought up.	
14.	My to-do list is endless.	
15.	I feel extremely guilty over some of the things I've done to others.	
16.	I often get myself into trouble, and then I punish myself for it.	
17.	It's better not to try than to risk failing.	

18.	I feel extremely anxious when things don't work out.	
19.	I feel embarrassed when I don't act according to others' expectations.	
20.	I often feel that if I were a better person, I would take better care of those I care about.	
21.	Sometimes I doubt whether I have the right to exist.	
22.	I think I'm too lazy to do anything important in my life.	
23.	Some of my habits make me feel ashamed.	
24.	I spend too much time on my projects in an attempt to make them perfect.	
25.	I fear that I'm a bad person.	
26.	I constantly avoid doing tasks.	

27.	I hate it when I can't be what my family expects of me.	
28.	I don't think I have what is needed to succeed.	

Once you've answered all the questions, follow the statements below to add your scores for the different types of inner critics. If you score higher than 9 per critic, your self-criticism is likely causing problems in your life. Scores of 7 or 8 may indicate some difficulties, while scores lower than 7, and especially 5, show you have a good handle on that type of inner critic:

- **Perfectionist:** Add your scores for questions 2, 11, 18, and 24

    - You set extremely high standards for yourself and are very harsh on yourself when you don't meet them.

- **Inner controller:** Add your scores for questions 3, 9, 16, and 23

    - You're often ashamed of your behavior and struggle with controlling your impulses.

- **Taskmaster:** Add your scores for questions 4, 14, 22, and 26

- You often give yourself negative labels in an attempt to motivate you to work harder.

- **Underminer:** Add your scores for questions 5, 10, 17, and 28

  - You're too scared to take risks out of fear of failure.

- **Destroyer:** Add your scores for questions 1, 6, 12, and 21

  - You struggle with low self-worth and often question the purpose of your life.

- **Guilt tripper:** Add your scores for questions 7, 15, 20, and 25

  - You easily feel guilty over your actions and feel like people will never forgive you for the mistakes you've made.

- **Molder:** Add your scores for questions 8, 13, 19, and 27

  - You're a people pleaser and will change aspects of yourself to try to please others.

Once you have a better understanding of the type of inner critic you have, you can work on improving those aspects of your life to increase your self-esteem and create the growth mindset you desire. The next stage on your journey to success is to make sure you understand the purpose of your life, or your "why."

Chapter 5:

Why Are You Doing This?

Our WHY is our purpose, cause, or belief—the driving force behind everything we do. –Simon Sinek

When you work on making any changes in your life— whether it's to develop a growth mindset, reduce self-criticism, or set healthy boundaries—you will encounter challenges along the way. To overcome them, it's important that you are aware and constantly remind yourself why you need to make these changes in your life.

This is what Carl, a 42-year-old father of two, had to learn the hard way. He was stuck in a dead-end job as a supervisor at a small engineering firm. While he earned a good salary and could provide for his family, he didn't feel challenged at work and, as a result, dreaded going to the factory. He decided to send his résumé to a few business contacts but never went over to actively apply for something else. Instead, he came up with one excuse after another, blaming others for his own unhappiness. He became very distracted at work and struggled to get up in the morning. He became highly irritated and stressed and made simple mistakes.

After hitting rock bottom, he decided to reach out to a mentor for advice. This mentor helped him understand that he didn't feel satisfied at work and that to get his life back on track, he needed to find his "why." After he took some time to re-evaluate his life, he finally came to the decision to find a job that matched his "why." Before long, Carl was in a new position. He loved his new job and excelled. Work didn't feel like work anymore. He went from dreading getting up in the morning to being excited to go to work.

Understanding the "why," or the purpose behind making the changes, helped Carl improve his life and health. You can do the same by identifying your why, changing some of your unhealthy habits, setting the right goals, and using if-then plans to deal with uncertainties more effectively.

The Importance of Knowing Your Why

Knowing your "why," or the purpose of your life, will help to bring a great deal of positivity to help you push through with the changes you need to make. It will help ensure that your actions are directly aligned with your goals, beliefs, and values. This will help you complete your tasks a lot quicker and easier, bring more happiness to your life, and let you see mistakes as opportunities to grow and improve rather than failures. Other benefits of knowing your "why" include:

- **You'll be more focused:** When you understand what the reasons are for doing something, it will be easier to pay attention to only what's important and take the necessary actions to reach your goals.

- **You'll be more passionate and committed:** Knowing why you're doing something and what benefits you'll gain from doing it will help push you to do whatever you can to reach your goals.

- **You'll have more clarity:** Having a deep understanding of what you need to do and why you need to do something can make you unstoppable in your efforts to reach your goals.

- **You'll enjoy life more:** When you know you're on the right path to reach your goals, you'll feel more fulfilled and satisfied with your life, which will help you find more enjoyment in your life.

- **You'll experience more trust:** The closer you get to your goals, the more you'll trust yourself and your own abilities. And when people see you achieving what you set out to do, their trust in you will also increase.

The Truths About Habits

Understanding the importance of knowing your "why" will help you identify the habits you have that don't serve this purpose, and therefore, you should work at breaking. Habits are the actions you take every day without thinking about it: You've been doing them repeatedly, and as a result, they've become automated. To help you understand habits, let's look at some interesting facts about them (*Psychology of Habits*, n.d.):

- About 40% of your actions are the result of habits, not conscious decisions.

- It takes around 66 days to break a bad habit.

- Habits can never be completely removed from your life, but you can overpower them with other habits.

- In order to create a habit, your brain has to crave it.

Now, let's look at how habits are formed. When you repeat the same action daily, you are creating a habit. Think about your morning routine. If you have coffee shortly after waking up, you've created a habit. If you brush your teeth after eating breakfast, you've created a habit. If you make your bed every morning, you've created a habit. The list goes on. You didn't simply wake up one day with these behaviors. You taught yourself over time to do them until they became so automated that you did them without thinking about them. It relies on using a three-step loop:

- **Cue:** This is the trigger that tells your brain what habit you should use.

- **Routine:** This is the actual behavior that you do when a habit forms.

- **Reward:** This is what your brain gets out of making the habit.

When you create healthy habits, you're essentially increasing your brain's efficiency, as you won't have to think while doing mundane tasks, freeing up your brain to focus on completing more important tasks. Let's look at an example: When you're feeling stressed (cue), going for a run (routine) will help you relax (reward).

While some habits can be healthy—such as brushing your teeth or working out—others can be very harmful to your health (such as smoking or drinking) or keep you from working toward your goals. These can include binge-watching a series while you're supposed to be working or procrastinating on important tasks. Let's go back to our example of feeling stressed and look at how your reaction can manifest into a bad habit: When you're feeling stressed (cue), smoking a cigarette (routine) will help you to calm down (reward).

If you want to change this bad habit, it will be extremely difficult to simply stop, as your brain is programmed into this loop and will continue to push you back into it. While you can force your brain to break this loop, it will be a lot more difficult than when you create a new loop that will give you the same reward, such as going for a jog or doing deep breathing exercises. Yes, in the beginning, you'll have to make a conscious decision every time you opt for the healthier loop, but over time it will get stronger, and your healthier option will become your automatic choice.

While creating a new loop is easier said than done, the following steps can help:

- **Look at your routine:** What behaviors do you want to change? What makes you do these behaviors? This step is very important, as it gives you the insights you need into the behavior you want to change.

- **Consider the reward:** What rewards does this habit give you? Is it a true escape from your struggles or simply a distraction? What negative consequences do you have as a result of this behavior? Now, think about what other habits you can introduce that will give you the same positive reward but without the negative consequences.

- **Identify your cue:** What triggers you to engage in this behavior? How did you react to these triggers before you learned this habit? How can you remind yourself to do a different thing when you experience this trigger?

Always remember that no matter how difficult it may be to break a bad habit, it is something that you can learn to control instead of allowing it to control you. It may also happen that, after trying for a while, your new (replacement) healthier habit doesn't work for you or give you the same reward as your old bad habit used to. If this happens, repeat the exercise above again to identify a different replacement habit. Make sure you're completely satisfied with your new habit, as this will make the process of breaking your old one a lot easier. Continue practicing this new habit and focusing on your why until your brain creates a new, strong pathway.

The Last Deadly P

In the previous chapter, we discussed two of the three deadly Ps: perfectionism and people-pleasing. Now, we'll discuss the third one: procrastination. Before we get into it, let's first get an important myth out of the way: Procrastinating doesn't necessarily mean you're lazy. Sure, some people will put off working on a specific task because they don't feel like it or rather want to do something they enjoy more. This isn't the case for everyone. Many people procrastinate so that their intense focus—often called hyperfocus—can kick in when the task becomes urgent, helping them to deliver their best work.

Regardless of what your reasons for procrastinating may be, always keep in mind that when you put off your tasks until the last minute, you will experience negative consequences such as stress, anxiety, exhaustion, and even disappointment. Even if your hyperfocus helps you deliver high-quality work, it can increase your risk of making mistakes, as you won't have enough time to go over your work to fix them. You also won't leave yourself enough time to deal with unplanned events such as illness, injury, or potential technical problems.

Many times, procrastination is linked to complex psychological reasons. It is often a self-protection mechanism where you can use the little time you have to complete the task as an excuse for not getting your desired results. By doing this, your capabilities can never be questioned, and your inner critic won't have anything negative to say. However, as much as this can reduce your risk of feeling "stupid," it can also increase your stress and anxiety levels, which can have damaging effects on your physical and mental health.

Let's look at ways you can overcome your habit of procrastination:

- **Know your why:** Ask yourself what the real reasons are for your procrastination. If you can become more aware of your why, you can work on the real cause of your procrastination instead of just working through the consequences.

- **Manage your time effectively:** Make sure you use the right techniques to manage your time. If you create long to-do lists or schedule tasks for every minute of your day, you may actually increase your anxiety and stress, which can lead to more procrastination. However, if you break your tasks up into small, achievable goals and allow yourself some flexibility in reaching them, you'll be more likely to push through and complete them.

- **Find productive motivation:** Make sure you know what the real benefits will be from completing a task. As much as you may find motivation in knowing that it's part of your job to complete a task, this reason alone may create negative emotions and hamper your ability to do what needs to be done. However, if you find deeper motivation—such as setting yourself up for a promotion at work—you'll create something that you can look forward to, which can bring amazing positivity to the task.

- **Make it exciting:** The more excited you are about doing something, the more willing you'll be to do whatever you can to complete it. Even the most boring and mundane tasks can be made more exciting. For example, if your task doesn't require a lot of concentration, consider listening to a podcast while you do it to keep you entertained or create some sort of reward for yourself for completing different aspects of your task.

Setting Goals

We've mentioned the importance of setting realistic and achievable goals, but you may wonder how you can go about doing it. To help you with this, let's first look at what a goal actually is. Some people might say their goal is to one day win a golf tournament or eventually gain financial freedom. These are not true goals but rather dreams for your life.

A goal, on the other hand, is a dream with a deadline and a set plan for how you will achieve it. For example, if you plan on training every day for the next six months to win the golf tournament this year or to invest a set amount of savings every month to gain your first level of financial freedom in two years' time, you're starting to set achievable goals with measurable objectives (your specific steps) and are well on your way to turning your dreams into a reality. It will give you a sense of control over and direction in your life and help you understand the bigger picture, not only of your life but also of the various steps you need to take.

Depending on the type of work you do or the relationships you have, you may have to set both personal and team goals. While you may take different steps in identifying and setting your personal and team goals, there are two important constants that you need to consider regardless of the type of goal you're setting: Your goal must be important enough to you that you want to achieve it, and it must be realistic. If you've never picked up a golf club before in your life, it will be completely unrealistic to expect to win a golf tournament in six months' time.

Let's look at three tips for setting personal goals:

- **Make sure you're passionate about it:** If you set goals that you aren't passionate about or truly want to achieve, you won't be motivated to do whatever you can to reach them.

- **Make sure your goals are within your control:** If you set goals that are dependent on the actions of others, you won't have control over whether you achieve your goals. This is why it's so important to carefully consider each goal you want to set and make sure it is realistic and achievable.

- **Think about the benefits:** Imagine how your life will be once you reach your goals and gain your benefits. This will help to motivate you to work toward reaching your goals so that you can gain these benefits.

While these tips can also be helpful when you create team goals, you need to consider all the other people and their personal goals when you do this:

- **Brainstorm**: Sit together with your team to discuss what everyone wants to achieve. Write down everything, as this can lead you to goals you haven't considered before.

- **Consider everyone**: Make sure everyone has a chance to voice their opinions, not only on the goals you want to achieve but also on the objectives you will set to reach these goals. If everyone gets the chance to give their input, they'll be more invested in doing what needs to be done to reach the team's goals.

- **Know the why**: As with all other goals, make sure everyone in the team understands the purpose of these goals and why it's important that they do their part in reaching them.

Even if you follow the tips above, it can still be difficult to go from goal-setting to goal-getting. There may be times when you feel overwhelmed and want to give up.

If this ever happens to you, the following tips can help you stay on track:

- **Set SMART goals**: Always make sure your goals are specific, measurable, achievable, realistic, and time-bound, as this will not only encourage you to push yourself toward reaching your goals but will also give you deadlines and ways to measure your success.

- **Write them down**: When you write your goals down, you'll be more committed to reaching them than when you think about them. It will also be easier to remind yourself of your goals, especially when you post them somewhere in your home or office where you will constantly see them.

- **Chunk it down**: If you have a big goal, you might easily be overwhelmed by its enormity. If you break this goal down into smaller goals or objectives, it will be less overwhelming.

- **Take action**: No matter how good your goals are or how well you've planned, you won't get anywhere if you don't take the necessary action to achieve them.

- **Create balance**: When you work toward a goal that you deeply want to achieve, you may go over and above what you're capable of, which can lead to burnout. Always make sure you have a balanced life and that you have enough time to rest.

- **Identify challenges**: It's unrealistic to expect that you won't face any challenges in reaching your goals. This is why it's important that you identify any obstacles you may face and plan how you'll overcome them.

- **Revisit your goals**: While you're busy working on your objectives to reach your goals, you may realize that some of these goals may not actually be what you want. When this is the case, it's important that you revisit and adjust them as you go to ensure that you have the right goals in your life.

If–Then Plans

As we've mentioned above, it's important that you consider any challenges you may face in reaching your goals so that you can plan how you will overcome them. A great way of doing this is by creating if-then plans, as you'll deliberately think of different scenarios as well as how you'll react in each of these situations, which will help you stay on the right path to reach your goals.

If-then plans are exactly as the name suggests. You'll think of a specific situation and plan what you'll do if it happens. Let's look at an example of having a goal of buying your first house in four years' time. You may set an objective of saving $100 every month until you have a deposit for this house.

Your if-then plans may look something like this:

- If I urgently need money, then I'll remind myself that my house savings are untouchable.

- If I can't save the full $100 in a month, then I will transfer as much as I can to my savings account and try to make up for what I'm behind on as soon as possible.

- If, after two years, I haven't reached half of my planned savings, then I will re-evaluate my plan to see how I can increase my savings.

- If I get an increase at work during this time, then I'll adjust my savings accordingly.

- If, after four years, I don't have enough money saved for a deposit, then I'll revisit my plan and decide if I'll opt for a cheaper apartment or continue to save for a house.

Let's look at another example of if-then plans. In this case, the goal will be to finish an important project a week before the deadline. Your if-then plans may look something like this:

- If I get distracted by a colleague, then I'll politely explain that I'm working on this project and request that they leave me alone.

- If I need more resources for this project, then I'll explain the situation to my boss and request additional resources.

- If the office gets too noisy for me to concentrate, then I'll move to a quiet corner.

- If I encounter any difficulties while busy with this project, then I'll immediately discuss them with my manager to get their advice on how to overcome them.

- If I see that I won't meet my deadline, then I'll discuss this with my superior to explain and request an extension.

Chapter 8:

How Do You Accept

Failure?

No man ever achieved worthwhile success who did not, at any time or other, find himself with at least one foot hanging well over the brink of failure. –Napoleon Hill

Every person has specific fears, whether it's fear of snakes, spiders, public speaking, ghosts, or even dying. While these are all legitimate fears, you might be surprised at how high the fear of not succeeding ranks. In a survey of 1,083 adults, 31% of them ranked the fear of failure as one of their top fears. This is more than the fear of spiders (30%), paranormal activity (15%), or being home alone (9%) (Moline, 2015).

Unfortunately, failure is something that can't be avoided. Whenever you try something new to improve your life, you run the risk of making mistakes. And if you decide not to make the necessary changes to your life out of fear of failing, you'll miss out on many opportunities in your life. This is why it's so important to understand that to reach any form of success, you'll likely have to deal with some degree of failure and that you can overcome any failure and turn it into massive wins on your journey to success.

The Fear of Failure

Before we get into how you can overcome your fear of failure, let's look at what this actually is. The simplest explanation of failure is not succeeding in doing something, so, therefore, fear of failure would be being scared of not succeeding. This can result in you staying in your comfort zone, procrastinating on your important tasks, and trying to blame others. You could have this fear over any part of your life: You might fear you won't have a successful marriage, so you avoid serious relationships. You may fear being a bad parent, so you decide you won't have children, or you may fear not being good at your job, so you stay stuck in a dead-end job that simply pays the bills instead of going for your dream job.

To start the process of overcoming your fear of failure, it's important to find the cause of it. Be patient with yourself as you work on identifying the cause of your fear. You may experience high levels of anxiety while you do this. However, if you're able to push through and not become overwhelmed, it will be absolutely worth it. While everyone's fear of failure may have different causes, the most common ones are:

- **Your childhood:** If you were brought up in a house where your caregivers were extremely critical of your actions and handed out severe punishments for mistakes, you might develop a fear of failure.

- **Being bullied:** If you were ever teased for making a mistake or not being good enough to make a specific team or get the job you applied for, you might avoid putting yourself out there due to a fear of this happening again and, as a result, sabotage yourself.

- **Traumatic events:** If you experience a traumatic event, you may avoid putting yourself in any situation or position that may result in this happening again. It can even make you hesitant to set long-term goals, particularly if this means trying something new.

- **Low self-esteem:** If you don't believe in yourself and your own abilities, you may think that regardless of how hard you try, you're only capable of failing, which can result in you avoiding any form of task out of your fear of failing.

Take some time to think about your life and the fears of failure you may have. Write them down in as much detail as you can, as this will be extremely helpful when you start to address these fears and work on strategies to overcome them.

Once you have a list of your fears, consider how they are affecting you and your ability to move forward in life. To help you with this, ask yourself these questions:

- Am I avoiding tasks because I am afraid of failing?

- Do I feel powerless when I have to do certain things?

- Are there specific tasks that make me feel anxious?

- How often do I feel like I've lost control?

- How do I feel when I fail at something?

- What are the actual consequences of failing? Are they aligned with my perceived consequences?

- Were my expectations and objectives realistic and achievable?

- What benefits can I get from failing?

The last three questions are very important on your journey to overcome your fear of failure. Many times, it can happen that your fear is so great that you overestimate the impact of any consequences you may face if you fail. When you take a step back and truly evaluate the impact, you may realize that this failure holds much less power and that the consequences aren't as severe as you feared them to be.

Then, when you fail at something, it's important that you reflect on whether your aim was realistic. While you should do this before you set your goals, you may only realize that your goal or objectives were unachievable once you've failed at them, as then factors you didn't consider before will become more apparent.

Lastly, any form of failure will have benefits. When you adopt a growth mindset, you'll see any mistakes as opportunities to learn. Therefore, all your failures will give you new insights into your problems and push you to think of different solutions. You don't have to become fearless. Fear is unavoidable. Instead, you need to develop the courage to take on tasks that will bring you closer to your goals despite being afraid and continue to take small, consistent steps.

Failure Is Part of Success

As we've mentioned, it's impossible to go through life without failing at some point or another. Failure is not just necessary; it's a stepping stone to something much greater and a vital aspect of achieving the success you desire. You might not immediately see it this way, especially if you've failed at something very recently, but over time, the reason for the failure will become clearer.

Think about a failure in your life that stands out, whether you think you understand why you've failed or are still trying to figure out the reason. Now, while keeping that in mind, consider the following life lessons that every failure brings:

- **Experience**: When you fail at completing a task, you gain a new experience that you wouldn't normally go through. This experience will help you reflect on what's truly important and teach you to let go of things that don't matter in your life.

- **Knowledge**: If you're open to learning lessons from your failures, you'll gain valuable knowledge that you can use to avoid future failures and propel you to even greater success.

- **Resilience**: Every time you get back up after failing, you increase your resilience. The stronger your resilience gets, the easier it will be to overcome failures in the future.

- **Growth**: Every time you fail, you gain experience, knowledge, and resilience. This will help you grow as a person and reach a new understanding of how the world works, what you value in life, and what you can do to improve it.

Failures bring a new perspective to your life that is otherwise difficult to gain.

- **Value**: With everything you do, you bring value not only to your life but also to those around you. Always think about your value and how much you've put into your task. You may discover that what you put in isn't equal to the results you wanted to achieve. This will help you create a better balance between your inputs and desired outcomes.

Once you've worked through the lessons you can learn from your failure, let's look at how you can recover from it and make sure you gain the maximum amount of value from it to achieve success in the future. The following tips can help you speed up your recovery from failure:

- **Ignore negative people**: When you fail, there will always be people who say something like, "If you listened to me, you wouldn't be in this predicament," "I told you so," or "Next time, ask me before you do something stupid." Ignore these people as much as you can. They don't bring any value to your life, and their words won't help you recover from your failure.

- **You can fail; just don't give up**: Everyone fails, but the difference between failures and winners is their reactions to this event. If you give up, you won't succeed and reach your goals. But if you push through, regardless of how difficult it may be, you will gain experience, knowledge, resilience, growth, and value, and you will reach success. Remember, failure is only failure if you give up.

- **Use failure as leverage**: When you fail at something, you can use this as a foundation on which your future success will be built. Try your best to understand the reasons why you failed and what you should do differently next time. Use this knowledge as a foundation for your success.

- **Rethink your goals**: Sometimes your failures can be a result of setting the wrong goals. You have to make sure that you set SMART goals and that you truly believe that reaching them will improve your life. If you aren't invested in your goals, you may struggle to reach them.

- **Create an action plan**: Make sure that you don't just plan your goals and objectives but also plan for failure. Plan for the worst-case scenarios, as then you'll know exactly what you want to do and how you want to do it to turn your perceived failure into something positive.

Finding Gratitude From Failure

As you develop your growth mindset and start to see your failures as opportunities for learning and growing, you'll understand that there's always something you can be grateful for. Being grateful not only helps you seek out the positives in life, but it also gives you the energy you need to push past your difficulties. It's about leaving any sense of entitlement you may have at the door and being grateful for every opportunity you may get, regardless of how negative it may seem. It's about seeing these negative situations (or failures) as opportunities to learn and grow.

Becoming more grateful takes continuous and consistent effort. You won't wake up one day and decide to live a life of gratitude. But you can teach your brain to become more aware of all the good things in your life. The more you practice it and acknowledge things in your life that you're grateful for, the easier this will become.

Think about a time in your life when you really struggled but overcame the obstacle you faced. Pay attention to the emotions you experienced while you were struggling. Now, focus on how you overcame that struggle and how you felt knowing that you didn't allow this negative experience to take control of your life. Did you allow your misery to take control over your life, or did you rise above it? Next, name five things from that experience that you're grateful for. Do you now see how easy it can be to focus on the positives? Yes, you focused on an experience that had a positive result, but by actively seeking out the positives in that situation, you're training your brain to seek out the good in any negative situation you may still encounter.

Let's look at other ways you can become more grateful:

- **Keep a gratitude journal:** Create a habit where every night before you go to bed, you write down at least three things that you're grateful for. While you can simply say these out loud, writing them down will give you a nice reference point for when you're experiencing difficulties, as you'll be able to page through the book to remind yourself of how much you actually have to be grateful for.

- **Connect with one person daily:** Make sure you connect with at least one person every day. Whether this is your partner, your child, your roommate, your coworker, or the person who works at the grocery store, make a connection, and share a joke so that you can laugh together.

- **Smile and laugh:** Adding to the previous one, laughter and smiling can be amazing tools to overcome negativity in your life. When you're feeling down, find something to laugh about, even if you have to search for a silly video online. When you smile or laugh, your body releases feel-good hormones and endorphins to improve your mood.

- **Counter a negative with a positive:** Every time you have a negative thought, counter it with a positive one. It's as simple as that. For example, when you think, "I hate my job," counter with, "I'm lucky to have a job."

Self-Assessment: Gratitude

Let's look at the failures of your life, how you were able to overcome them, and what you're most grateful for. Answer each of the questions below honestly and in as much detail as you can. This will help you put the learnings from this chapter directly into practice:

What was one of the biggest struggles you had to overcome?

What did you learn in terms of:

Experience:	Knowledge:	Resilience:	Growth:	Value:

Name three things you're grateful for in your personal life:

Today:	Yester day:	Past week:	Past month:	Past year:

Name three things you're grateful for in your professional life:

Today:	Yester-day:	Past week:	Past month:	Past year:

Name three things you will do tomorrow to be positive:

Failing is unavoidable, and often you don't have much control over it. However, what you can control is how you choose to react and apply your growth mindset to seek out opportunities to learn. You can turn your failures into foundations on which you build your future success. You can create the life you've always wanted. You can live a life filled with gratitude and opportunities. You can *change your mindset to achieve success.*

Self-Assessment: Know Your Why

The secret to making changes to improve your life and reach your goal is understanding why you're doing it. If you understand the purpose of each change, you'll be motivated to do what you can to turn your goals into reality. To help you with this, answer the questions in the self-assessment below truthfully (Byrne, 2020):

What aspects of your life do you want to change?
Why do you want to make these changes?

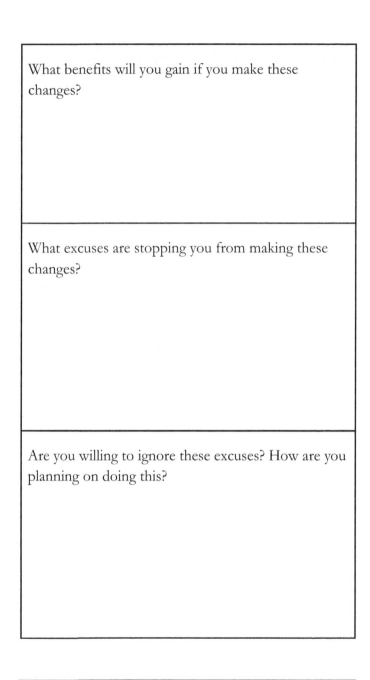

What benefits will you gain if you make these changes?

What excuses are stopping you from making these changes?

Are you willing to ignore these excuses? How are you planning on doing this?

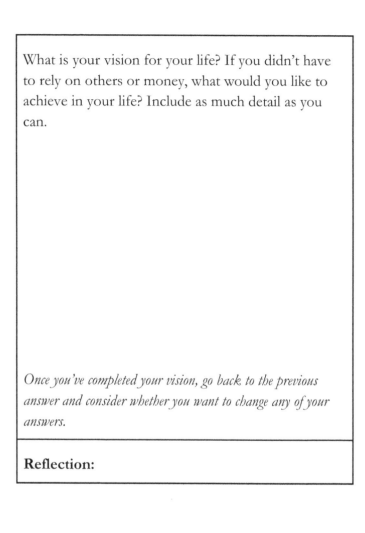

What is your vision for your life? If you didn't have to rely on others or money, what would you like to achieve in your life? Include as much detail as you can.

Once you've completed your vision, go back to the previous answer and consider whether you want to change any of your answers.

Reflection:

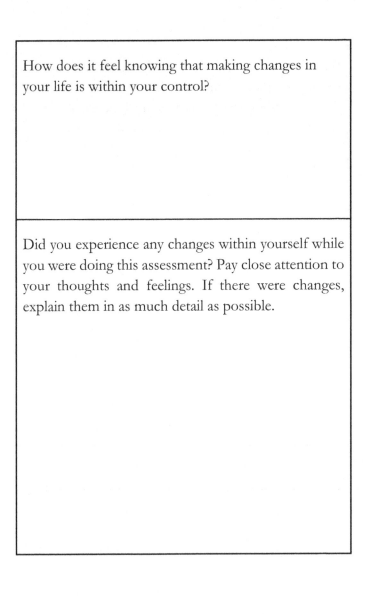

How does it feel knowing that making changes in your life is within your control?

Did you experience any changes within yourself while you were doing this assessment? Pay close attention to your thoughts and feelings. If there were changes, explain them in as much detail as possible.

You can achieve anything you want in life if you understand and use the incredible power within you. Make sure you always know and remember your why, as this will make it easier for you to not only make the necessary changes in your life but also push you to reach your goals. Unfortunately, being motivated isn't always enough to keep you going. In the next chapter, we'll discuss what you can do when motivation isn't enough to help you reach your goals.

Chapter 6:

What If Motivation Is Not

Enough?

The world's greatest achievers have been those who have always stayed focused on their goals and have been consistent in their efforts. –Dr. Rooplen

Knowing why you need to make certain changes to your life and how they will benefit you is a fantastic tool for keeping you motivated to reach your goals. However, there are times when motivation alone just isn't enough.

This is what Jane, a 55-year-old business owner, learned. She has a team of 15 employees at her creative agency. Despite being a small business, they took on big projects for international brands. As a result, she pushed her employees to sometimes work harder than is humanly possible, and she rewarded them accordingly with time off between projects. For many years, this motivation was effective, and her staff gave their best. However, some of her employees started to become unmotivated by this reward. Soon, this created a snowball effect where more and more staff members started expressing their unwillingness to push themselves as they had in the past.

In discussions to find the cause of the problem, Jane discovered that her staff didn't feel invested in the company. They appreciated the reward she offered but felt it wasn't enough motivation. They wanted to feel like she was invested in them as people and not just see them as employee numbers she had to pay. Jane took their complaints on board and offered her staff skill development programs. Some of the courses she offered her staff were outsourced, while she provided most of the training herself. This development didn't break the bank and afforded her more time with her staff. She also created a recognition system where an employee of the week is chosen, who would then choose what takeout food the entire office would enjoy together on a Friday. Jane created a rule that no matter how busy they are, they will spend at least the lunch hour together on a Friday, eating a meal and getting to know each other better.

This serves as a far greater motivator for her staff than the traditional reward. Jane's staff spoke up about what would help them improve their work. And Jane thought of new ways of encouraging her staff to be motivated again. Similarly, you need to not only speak up—even just to your own inner critic—about what you need but also come up with ways to keep going, no matter how unmotivated you may be.

Motivation Is Not Enough

While being motivated is a fantastic tool to get closer to your goals, it is a temporary state. No one will be motivated to continue with every task they take on until it's completed, and no other person can motivate you if you don't allow them to. They can encourage you to keep at it, but if you aren't willing to do something, they can't motivate you. To help you understand this, let's look at the two traditional drivers of motivation:

- **Away motivation:** This is when you're trying to get away from someone or a situation. Your fears will take priority in this type of motivation, and it will only remain in place as long as you have a specific fear or problem.

- **Towards motivation:** This is when you're working towards a specific goal that will improve your life. Once you've reached this goal, this motivation will be lost, and you'll need to find a new goal to recreate it.

Both of these types of motivation are based on external factors, and your motivation will disappear as soon as these factors are no longer present. They start out with trying to fulfill a basic need and end once you've reached this new level of power or achievement. If you can eliminate the need for external factors to become motivated and focus on becoming inspired by your internal guidance, you won't need to seek external, temporary motivation anymore. You will feel inspired to do certain tasks and will act according to your inspiration.

If you are wondering what inspired action looks like, here are a few characteristics that you can try to incorporate into your life:

- Always seeking the silver lining in every dark cloud.

- Detach your self-worth from the outcomes of any actions.

- Want what is best, not just for yourself but also for others.

- Seek clarity before you take action.

- Live in the present without overly worrying about the future.

- Understand who you really are and what you want in life.

- Act with enthusiasm, gratitude, and appreciation.

While motivation can be a great tool in reaching your goals, seeking out inspiration so you can act with an inspired state of mind will help you achieve the success you desire, even when you lack the motivation you may have thought you needed.

Willpower Can Be Depleted

Now that we've discussed the importance of seeking out inspiration in combination with motivation; let's look at willpower. This inner strength often has many different names, such as resilience, self-control, self-discipline, determination, and resolve, and comes down to the following:

- Waiting for gratification by resisting temptations while focusing on achieving long-term goals.

- Regulating yourself by fighting off unwanted and negative thoughts and impulses.

- Thinking through problems instead of reacting in an emotional state.

Apart from the above, your willpower will help you push through when you have to do unpleasant tasks and let you get back at it if you stumble and fall along the way. Unfortunately, no one has an endless supply of willpower. Think of your willpower as a muscle. You use this muscle (or willpower) every day for many different tasks you need to do, such as working instead of surfing the web or choosing to work out instead of lying on the couch. The more you use this muscle, the stronger it will get. However, if you overuse it, it may result in muscle fatigue or even muscle strains. So, just like your muscle can suffer serious damage if you don't rest it, your willpower can also get depleted. Similarly, just like you can do specific exercises to strengthen a muscle, you can also increase your willpower by doing the following:

- **Learn to manage stress**: When you're experiencing high levels of stress, your body will use all its energy to fight off the perceived threat, and most of your decisions will be to create short-term outcomes instead of focusing on the more important long-term goals. Whenever you feel overwhelmed, practice deep breathing or do a quick meditation session to find calm.

- **Stop saying "I can't"**: Whenever you say negative words such as "I can't" or "I don't," you're limiting your own capabilities, as your brain will believe that you aren't capable of these things when, in reality, you may simply not want to do something. Instead, be honest with yourself by saying something like, "Even though I may not feel like doing this now, I can do it."

- **Give your brain energy**: Whenever you don't get enough sleep, you are depleting your brain of the energy it needs to effectively fulfill its functions. Make sure you get good rest every night by reducing your use of electronics at least

30 minutes before you want to fall asleep, making sure your room is dark and cool, and not eating sweet treats close to your bedtime. If you find yourself struggling to fall asleep, get up and read a book for about 20 minutes to help boost your body's creation of melatonin, the hormone that helps you fall asleep.

- **Look after your body**: Make sure you eat healthy, nutritious food and get exercise daily. This has a direct impact on your brain's prefrontal cortex, which influences your ability to make decisions. Apart from this, exercise also releases feel-good hormones and endorphins, which will boost your willpower and your ability to push through unpleasant tasks.

- **Focus only on what's important now**: How often do you find yourself distracted by things that may be important later but not now? This takes your attention away from the important tasks that are urgent, which can increase your stress levels.

- **Don't take on too much**: When it comes to setting objectives and goals, make sure you focus on one at a time. This will help you feel in control of your life and, as a result, boost your willpower to push through with the task until it's done.

- **Avoid temptation**: This comes back to delaying your gratification. If you know you need to do something now, don't give in to any temptations you may experience along the way. By delaying gratification, you teach your body that you are capable of waiting for what you want, and you'll enjoy the reward (or gratification) a lot more if your important tasks are done.

Progress Is Greater Than Outcome

There may be times when you reach one goal after another, while other times you struggle to get a single task ticked off. Always be kind to yourself and remind yourself that any progress, regardless of how insignificant it may seem, is better than no progress. In many cases, your progress may also be more important than any results you may achieve. Just start—whether you take a small step or a giant leap, doing something is better than doing nothing.

Also, while the outcome will be your ultimate goal, the process you follow to get there may often be the most important part of your journey. Let's look at three reasons for this:

- **You can't get anywhere without a map:** If you don't have specific planned steps on how you want to reach your goals, you won't get there, no matter how much you want to reach these outcomes. Think of your planned steps as a roadmap to your ideal destination. If you don't follow the map, you won't know which route you need to take or how to get there. But, by following your map, you can choose the best route to reach your destination safely and on time.

- **Focus only on the "now":** While you're following your roadmap to success, it's important that you pay full attention to every step you take to ensure that you complete it as best you can. You can't do that if your mind is distracted. Decide that you'll see every step on your journey as a big moment that deserves your full focus.

- **Always re-evaluate:** The progress that you make will be useless if you work on the wrong objectives or try to achieve the wrong goals. Always re-evaluate your processes and desired outcomes and adjust them whenever it's necessary. Think again of your process as a roadmap. On the route that you decide to take, you might encounter an unexpected roadblock. To reach your destination, you need to pick another route to take.

Self-Assessment: Your Goals

Let's now get you from goal setting to goal getting by evaluating your goals and the actionable steps, or objectives; you want to set in your life. Below is a space where you can write down five different goals, with five steps to take for each one. Make sure these steps are small and easily reachable, as this will help push you closer to reaching your desired outcomes. Once you've completed the table, decide which goal you want to work on first. Always remember to focus only on one goal at a time so that you can give it your full attention.

Goal 1	
Actionable steps	1.
	2.
	3.
	4.
	5.
Goal 2	
Actionable steps	1.
	2.
	3.
	4.
	5.
Goal 3	
Actionable	1.

steps	2.
	3.
	4.
	5.
Goal 4	
Actionable steps	1.
	2.
	3.
	4.
	5.
Goal 5	
Actionable steps	1.
	2.
	3.

	4.
	5.

You now understand that motivation alone might not always be enough to reach your goals. You also need to act with inspiration and constantly work on improving your willpower, and you should focus on your progress rather than your outcomes. When you take on big goals, it can be very helpful to break the task into smaller steps. In the next chapter, we'll discuss the immense impact that these small steps can have on your life.

Chapter 7:

How Do You Find

Greatness in the Tiny?

Great things are not done by impulse, but by a series of small things brought together. –Vincent van Gogh

Many people have misconceptions when it comes to the size of their dreams. They believe that just because their dreams and goals are big, their actions should be similarly big. However, this can result in you easily being overwhelmed by the enormity of your objectives, leading to you failing before you have even started.

Let's look at famous examples of how you can achieve greatness by taking tiny steps. Sir Richard Branson started his massive Virgin brand by publishing a student magazine. Amazon started by only selling books until founder Jeff Bezos expanded it into the multi-billion-dollar company it is today. And who can forget the humble beginnings of Apple? Steve Jobs and Steve Wozniak launched their tech giants from Jobs' garage.

These three giants in business dreamed big but started

with small enough steps that they could easily manage. Once they started to taste success, they expanded, one small step at a time. They didn't get overwhelmed by the size of their dreams or the steps they had to take to reach their goals. They proved the immense power that lies in starting small.

Starting Small Has Power

When you were a baby, you had to learn to take a few steps before you could walk and eventually run. As a toddler, you had to learn number recognition before you could do math. As a preschooler, you had to learn phonics before you could read. The key to success is to start small.

Think about it this way: If you commit to completing one big task a day, you'll complete seven in a week, 28 in a month, and 336 in a year. Now, let's turn that into five small tasks a day. You'll then complete 35 in a week, 140 in a month, and 1,680 in a year. Do you see the difference? Yes, you may argue that the benefits of completing these smaller tasks will be less than completing a big task, but it will also mean you'll achieve 1,344 more small victories in a year if you aim for completing smaller tasks.

While this in itself should already be a benefit that will

get most people hooked, let's look at five more:

- **It takes less energy and time**: A small task is easier to complete, while satisfaction will be similar regardless of the size of the task. What's more, the effect of these small victories will accumulate much quicker than that of bigger tasks.

- **It increases your confidence**: With every task you complete, your confidence and self-esteem will increase. You'll feel good about yourself, and this will drive you to want to complete more tasks.

- **It gives you the ability to improve**: With every small task you complete, you can get feedback, either by assessing the task yourself or asking others for their input. You can then use this feedback to improve how you go about completing your next task.

- **It's just the first step**: When you take on a new goal, you can only go about reaching it by taking one step at a time. Should you make a mistake on a small task, it won't have as big an impact on your overall outcome as if you made an error on a bigger step. It's also easier to fix a small mistake than a bigger one.

- **It doesn't define your dream**: No matter how big your dream is, you can go about reaching it by taking small steps. Just because you're taking baby steps doesn't mean your ultimate outcome will be small. Bezos started with baby steps, and his results with Amazon are by no means small. If you consistently take small steps, you will arrive at the destination of your choice.

Small Achievements Create Momentum

A key principle of success is creating momentum that will push your progress to the next level. By taking small steps, you'll consistently achieve victories that will propel your momentum forward. These victories will give you the confidence to discuss your goals and objectives with others, as you'll be able to explain the amazing results you've already achieved. This can result in them sharing their ideas with you, which can increase your results even more. Your small achievements will also increase your understanding of your goals and put you in a much better position to adjust your objectives where necessary to ensure you reach your desired results.

Here is an example of a 90-day exercise you can use to help you create the correct momentum:

- Take a sheet of paper and write down the goal you want to achieve.

- Write a goal statement as if you've already reached it to show what you will achieve. Include some benefits of reaching this goal.

- List the different actions you will take to reach this goal. First, only focus on the first 30 steps. Think of one step you'll take each day for the next 30 days and commit to it.

- After 30 days, re-evaluate your progress. Think about what worked and what didn't. Identify any steps you may have missed or should include going forward.

- Discuss your goals with other people or your mentor. Get their input to create more objectives.

- Continue with your next steps for another 30 days and re-evaluate your goal and objections again.

- After 90 days, you will have completed 90 steps. Look at your results. If you've reached your goal, congratulate yourself! You are allowed to be proud. If you're not there yet, don't be too hard on yourself. Simply identify what your next steps should be and push ahead for another 30 days.

Consistency

Another key principle to success is consistency. As we've discussed, it's the driving force behind the momentum that you'll create by taking small steps daily. To be consistent in something, you need to be disciplined and dedicate yourself long-term until the goal has been reached. While distractions and giving in to your impulses can divert your focus from what is really important in your life, consistently making an effort to complete small tasks will get you closer to reaching the success you desire. Other reasons why consistency is key include:

- **It creates accountability**: When you set objectives for yourself, you accept accountability for your own actions. If you fail to complete a task, you'll only have yourself to blame. You'll also know exactly what task you missed and that you need to make time to complete it if you want to reach your goal.

- **It creates trust**: You'll increase the trust you have in yourself as you prove to yourself daily that you're capable of completing your tasks. Other people will also notice your effort and see that you're doing what you set out to do. This creates credibility, which will lead them to trust you as well. This, in turn, can boost your self-confidence and create even more momentum.

- **It increases self-control**: It's easy to give in to impulses or allow yourself to be distracted. However, if you push yourself to consistently complete tasks, you'll develop strong self-control and become more disciplined in your actions.

- **It creates measurable goals**: With every task you complete, your goal will become more measurable. You'll not only know exactly how far you are from reaching your goal, but you'll also be able to determine whether your goal is realistic and make adjustments based on facts.

Everyone is capable of becoming more consistent in completing tasks, but in reality, life can get in the way. You may get sick and be unable to complete a task, or you may have to wait for resources before you can continue. While these two examples are things that aren't in your control, you can work on managing your internal factors to keep you going:

- **Set reminders:** When you're busy with other tasks, you might forget about the specific objective you set out for that day. To avoid this, it can be helpful to set reminders, for example, on your phone or Post-its.

- **Reward yourself:** After you've completed your task for the day, you can reward yourself. This doesn't have to mean something big. Even something as simple as allowing yourself one extra episode of your favorite series or having that sweet treat you've been craving can be a reward. By doing this, you'll acknowledge the work you've put in so far and inspire yourself to work just as hard on your next task.

- **Enjoy your results:** When you consistently work on completing small tasks or making changes to your life, you'll give yourself more time to appreciate and enjoy your results. This can be another great tool to motivate you to continue with your hard work.

- **Speak to a mentor:** Consistent work will help you identify any mistakes or obstacles in your plan. You can address these immediately and seek advice from your mentor before they become massive hurdles that slow your progress.

Self-Assessment: Monitor Your Progress

Tracking your progress is a very important part of working toward achieving your goals. By doing this, you'll always know exactly what you've done, what your next step should be, what steps still lie ahead of you, and what benefits you've gained thus far:

Goal:				
Objective:	Scheduled date:	Completed date:	Obstacles identified:	Benefits gained:

No matter how well you plan and execute your various objectives, you will likely encounter obstacles on your journey to success. When this happens, you have the choice of whether you're going to allow this obstacle to result in overall failure or whether you'll see this as a learning curve to improve yourself. In the last chapter, we'll discuss why failure is actually an important part of success and how you can deal with it.

Conclusion

You now have all the tools you need to break free from the shackles that have kept you from achieving success. You understand how low self-esteem and a fixed mindset can make it seem impossible to reach your goals and that to work on moving to a growth mindset, you need to accept yourself and embrace the changes you need to make to move out of your comfort zone. You also know how to recognize the ANTs in your life and overcome your limiting beliefs.

Once you are able to let go of these ANTs, you'll be able to befriend your inner critic and reduce your self-criticism to the point where you'll understand that you're worthy of setting healthy boundaries to not only protect yourself but also help your journey to success. Always remember your "why" in every change that you make, and make sure the goals you set are not only realistic and achievable but also important to you, as this will give you the motivation and inspiration to reach them. If you ever struggle, focus on the progress you've made so far and continue to create momentum by taking small steps toward your goal consistently.

There may be times when you fail. However, don't let your fear of failure keep you from going after what you want. See these failures as opportunities to learn, grow, and remember to reflect on your journey with gratitude for how far you've come.

Changing your mindset and gearing yourself for success may not be as easy as it sounds, but it can definitely be done. Use the lessons you learned from the book, move from a fixed mindset to a growth mindset, and start carving your path to success.

I wish you all the best on your journey to a better life filled with the success you desire.

If you found the content in the book helpful, please leave a review on Amazon so that I can help others achieve success.

References

Abel, A. (2022, May 26). *Why embracing change is essential to growth.* Smaller Earth. https://www.smallerearth.com/uk/blog/why-embracing-change-is-essential-to-growth

About self-esteem. (2022, August). Mind. https://www.mind.org.uk/information-support/types-of-mental-health-problems/self-esteem/about-self-esteem/

Alban, P. (2023, February 13). *Automatic negative thoughts (ANTs): How to break the habit.* Be Brain Fit. https://bebrainfit.com/automatic-negative-thoughts/

Aneva, D. (2022, June 30). *Why self-acceptance is the key to success.* CEO Today. https://www.ceotodaymagazine.com/2022/06/why-self-acceptance-is-the-key-to-success/

Bennett, R. T. (n.d.). *Mindset quotes.* GoodReads. https://www.goodreads.com/quotes/tag/mindset

Bertin, M. (2019, August 21). *A basic meditation to tame your inner critic.* Mindful.

https://www.mindful.org/basic-meditation-tame-inner-critic/

Byrne, D. (2020). *Self-care: Accepting ourselves for who truly are.* Deborah Byrne Psychology Services

Carol Dweck's growth versus fixed mindset assessment. (n.d.). SSB Performance. https://cdn2.sportngin.com/attachments/document/8ab2-2573672/Carol_Dwecks_Growth_vs._Fixed_Mindset.pdf

Cherry, K. (2023, February 13). *Common signs of low self-esteem.* Verywell Mind. https://www.verywellmind.com/signs-of-low-self-esteem-5185978

Coffman, M. (2020, May 15). *Gratitude is the antidote to failure.* Therapy Practice Accelerator. https://therapypracticeaccelerator.com/gratitude-is-the-antidote-to -failure/

Cooper, B. B. (2013, December 5). *6 ways to improve your willpower.* Buffer Resources. https://buffer.com/resources/willpower-and-the-brain-why-its-so- hard-to-avoid-temptation/

Covert, C. (2018, December 3). *3 reasons the process is more important than the outcome.* Medium. https://medium.com/@ChrisAchieve/3-

reasons-the-process   -is-more-important-than-
the-outcome-c7146a233bed

Curry, S. (n.d.). *Stephen Curry Quote*. A-Z Quotes.
https://www.azquotes.com/ quote/1458561

Curtis, C. (2020, August 18). *Embracing a growth mindset*.
The   Mom   Project.
https://blog.themomproject.com/embracing-a-
growth-mindset

Dweck, C. (2015, March 2). *Carol Dweck: A summary of the
two   mindsets*.   Farnam   Street.
https://fs.blog/carol-dweck-mindset/

*8 celebs who unexpectedly opened up about their insecurities and
made us love them even more*. (2022, February 26).
Bright Side — Inspiration. Creativity. Wonder.
https://brightside.me/wonder-people/7-
celebrities-who-struggled-with-low-self-esteem-
show-us-were-not-alone-805619/

Exercise   the   inner   critic   questionnaire.   (n.d.).
https://barriefht.ca/wp-content/uploads
/2019/10/7.-Exercise-the-Inner-Critic-
Questionnaire.pdf

Flip your focus: How you can change your mindset. (n.d.). Her
Culture.
https://www.herculture.org/blog/2021/2/11/f

lip-your-focus-how-you-can-change-your-mindset

Fostering a positive self-image. (2017). Cleveland Clinic. https://my.clevelandclinic. org/health/articles/12942-fostering-a-positive-self-image

Gallo, C. (2021, September 27). *5 cognitive biases blocking your success.* Forbes. https://www.forbes.com/sites/carminegallo/2021/09/27/5-cognitive-biases-blocking-your-success/?sh=42bb56842402

Gascoigne, J. (2014, March 6). *The habits of successful people: they start small.* Buffer Resources. https://buffer.com/resources/make-it-big-by-starting-small/

Glassman, C. F. (n.d.). *Negative thinking quotes.* GoodReads. https://www.goodreads.com/quotes/tag/negative-thinking

Glossinger, J. (2021, September 20). *How to be consistent and why it's important to your success.* Morning Coach. https://www.morningcoach.com/ blog/how-to-be-consistent-and-why-it-s-important-to-your-success

Goodman, L. (n.d.). *The limiting belief quiz.* http://creatingonpurpose.net/wp-content/

uploads/2013/01/The-Limiting-Belief-Quiz.pdf

Graham, R. (2021, July 26). *Is being a people pleaser holding you back from success.* Robyn Graham. https://therobyngraham.com/beingapeopleplea ser/

Grande, C. (2022, March 11). *Chloë's story: Free from self-criticism.* Libero. https://liberomagazine.com/stories/chloes-free-from-self-critique/

Growth mindset vs fixed mindset: Can mindset be changed? (2023, March 3). Aventis Learning. https://aventislearning.com/growth-mindset-for-individual-success/

Guttman, J. (2019, June 27). *The relationship with yourself.* Psychology Today. https://www.psychologytoday.com/intl/blog/s ustainable-life-satisfaction/201906/the-relationship-yourself

Hamptom, D. (2022, March 22). *Your mindset shapes your life - for better or worse.* The Best Brain Possible. https://thebestbrainpossible.com/mindset-growth- fixed-success-mental-health/

Hay, L. L. (n.d.). *Self-criticism quotes*. Good Reads. https://www.goodreads.com/ quotes/tag/self-criticism

Hill, N. (n.d.). *Napoleon Hill quotes*. BrainyQuote. https://www.brainyquote.com/ quotes/napoleon_hill_401711

Himot, O. (2022, July 2). *Creating momentum - A success principle.* LinkedIn. https://www.linkedin.com/pulse/creating-momentum-success-principle-oshana-himot-mba/?trk=pulse-article_more-articles_related-content-card

Jha, R. (2013, June 12). *Self acceptance - Key to Happiness.* WisdomTimes. https://www.wisdomtimes.com/blog/self-acceptance-key-to-happiness/

Kong, F. J. (2022, April 3). *Motivation alone is not enough.* Philstar. https://www.philstar.com/business/2022/04/03/2171795/motivation-alone-not-enough

Lattimer, C. (2020, January 7). *6 reasons why being motivated is not enough.* The People Development Magazine. https://peopledevelopmentmagazine.com/ 2020/01/07/being-motivated-is-not-enough/

Lim, S. (2020, November 7). *5 reasons why starting small is the key to success.* Addicted2Success. https://addicted2success.com/success-advice/5-reasons-why -starting-small-is-the-key-to-success/

Magosky, S. (2021, January 19). *How perfectionism is ruining your life.* The LeaderShift Project. https://theleadershiftproject.com/ls-articles/2073/

Manson, M. (2020, November 12). *How to overcome your limiting beliefs.* Mark Manson. https://markmanson.net/limiting-beliefs

Marcus, B. (2017, October 17). *How does a lack of confidence affect your life and career?* Forbes. https://www.forbes.com/sites/bonniemarcus/ 2017/10/17/how- does-a-lack-of-confidence-affect-your-life-and-career/?sh=40d73f2d1ac4

McCarthy, M. (2019, August 8). *Why strong self-esteem is the secret to success in life.* Create Write Now. https://www.createwritenow.com/journal-writing-blog/ why-strong-self-esteem-is-the-secret-to-success-in-life

Meacham, M. (2014, September 10). *The growth mindset starts in the brain.* Association for Talent

Development.   https://www.td.org/insights
/the-growth-mindset-starts-in-the-brain

Mindset.   (n.d.).   Cale   Learning   Enhancement.
https://inside.ewu.edu/calelearning/
psychological-skills/mindset/

Moline, P. (2015, October 31). *We're far more afraid of
failure than ghosts: Here's how to stare it down.* Los
Angeles   Times.   https://www.latimes.com/
health/la-he-scared-20151031-story.html

Murtaza, Q. (2014, July 24). *The shoes story.* LinkedIn.
https://www.linkedin.com/
pulse/20140724045621-56724952-the-shoes-
story-positive-thinking-negative-thinking-
attitude-perspective-mindset/

Naim, R. (2018, February 15). *When you learn to accept your
flaws,   you   thrive.*   Thought   Catalog.
https://thoughtcatalog.com/rania-
naim/2018/02/when-you- learn-to-accept-your-
flaws-you-thrive/

Patel, S. (2017, October 9). *7 lessons on failure you can learn
from   top   athletes.*   Entrepreneur.
https://www.entrepreneur.com/leadership/7-
lessons-on-failure   -you-can-learn-from-top-
athletes/300699

Psychology of habits. (n.d.). The World Counts. https://www.theworldcounts.com /purpose/psychology-of-habits

Rao, S. (2017, March 4). *96% of people fail when they try to better themselves — here are 3 ways to make sure you don't.* Business Insider. https://www.businessinsider.com/96-of-people-fail-when-they-try-to-better-themselves-here-are-3-ways-to-make-sure-you-dont-2017-3

Schaffner, A. K. (2020, October 15). *Living with your inner critic: 8 helpful worksheets and activities.* PositivePsychology. https://positivepsychology.com/ inner-critic-worksheets/

Schroeder, B. (2020, March 11). *Change is hard but unavoidable. Eight insights on embracing change.* Forbes. https://www.forbes.com/sites/bernhardschroe der/ 2020/03/11/change-is-hard-but-unavoidable-eight-insights-on-embracing-change/?sh=645cf412ec8f

Shah, N. (2019, November 14). *Consistency is the key to success: 6 simple actionable tips to develop.* ICHARS. https://instituteofclinicalhypnosis.com/self-help/ consistency-is-the-key-to-success/

Silver, N. (2022, May 27). *Can keeping a growth mindset increase your neuroplasticity?* Healthline. https://www.healthline.com/health/growth-mindset-neuroplasticity#encouraging-growth

Sinek, S. (n.d.). *Find your why quotes by Simon Sinek.* GoodReads. https://www.goodreads.com/work/quotes/49782500-find-your-why

The importance of failure: 5 valuable lessons from failing. (2019). Wanderlust Worker. https://www.wanderlustworker.com/the-importance-of-failure-5-valuable-lessons-from-failing/

Trueblood, S. (2014, May 31). *The 3 deadly P's: Perfectionism, procrastination, and people pleasing.* Austin Mindfulness. https://www.austinmindfulness.org/post/ the-3-deadly-p-s-perfectionism-procrastination-and-people-pleasing

Twenty questions to help you challenge negative thoughts. (n.d.). Northeastern Ohio Universities. https://www.mcgill.ca/counselling/files/counselling/20_questions _to_challenge_negative_thoughts_0.pdf

Van Gogh, V. (n.d.). *A quote by Vincent van Gogh.* GoodReads.

https://www.goodreads.com/quotes/75899-
great-things-are-not-done-by-impulse-but-by-a

Vien, T. (2019, July 10). *The progress is far more important than the result.* LinkedIn. https://www.linkedin.com/pulse/progress-far-more-important-than-result-dominic-thang/

Voge, D. (2007). *Understanding and overcoming procrastination.* McGraw Center for Teaching and Learning; Princeton University. https://mcgraw.princeton.edu/undergraduates/resources/resource-library/understanding-and-overcoming-procrastination

Waters, S. (2022, September 15). *Why do we fear failure? Understanding setbacks to conquer wins.* Better Up. https://www.betterup.com/blog/why-do-we-fear- failure

What you need to know about willpower: The psychological science of self-control. (2021). American Psychological Association. https://www.apa.org/topics/personality/willpower

Whitener, S. (2019, December 11). *How setting boundaries positively impacts your self-esteem.* Forbes. https://www.forbes.com/sites/forbescoachescouncil/2019/ 12/11/how-setting-boundaries-

positively-impacts-your-self-
esteem/?sh=6974d4bc339c

Why gratitude is the key to unlocking happiness and success.
(2019, September 22). Stepping Stones to FI.
https://steppingstonestofi.com/ gratitude-
happiness-success/

Wooll, M. (2022, February 7). *Self-criticism and how to
overcome it.* BetterUp.
https://www.betterup.com/blog/self-criticism

Zuleta, L. (2021, January 17). *The importance of knowing your
'why'.* LinkedIn.
https://www.linkedin.com/pulse/important-
know-your-why-lorena-zuleta/

Made in the USA
Las Vegas, NV
02 November 2023

80105647R00108